LIFE
IS
PREDICTABLE

SUNDAY ADELAJA

Sunday Adelaja
LIFE IS PREDICTABLE
©2018Sunday Adelaja
ISBN 978-1985858008

Copyright © Golden Truth Publishing
Kiev, Ukraine. All rights reserved
www.goldentruth.pro

Cover design by Alexander Bondaruk
Interior design by Olena Kotelnykova

© Sunday Adelaja, 2018,
Life Is Predictable — Kiev, Ukraine:
Golden Truth Publishing, 2018

TABLE OF CONTENTS

FROM THE AUTHOR

DEAR READER,

Life is given to everyone, but very few people under-stand it. Very few people take time to know the depths of life and learn how to have a quality life by living effectively. There are many stereotypes of deceit and lies about life, in the world around us. Many people think that they know everything about life, but in reality they are simply deceived.

I want to share with you, in this book you are holding in your hands, the truths about the laws of life from the Lord Jesus Christ, the One who knows life more than all of us. He teaches us that life is a lot more than how we imagine and think about it.

The devil does not want us to know that life is our only chance. Most of life's opportunities are given to us only once, just like life itself. It is impossible to redeem the time we have spent, so each of us must learn to value life, make every passing day a blessed and fruitful day to God and people. We must live a quality life, be successful, and manifest God's glory on this earth.

Try to get a deep insight about the truths that the Lord is revealing to you through this book, and remember that you should not live today, thinking that you have tomorrow. You only have today, and you are responsible for how you will use it. Learn to use the opportunities God has given you in life, and appreciate what you have today.

The quality of your life does not depend on your financial status, but on your personal relationship with the author of this life. Jesus Christ is *the way, the truth and the life* *(John 14:6)*. You can have a quality life in abundance here on earth and eternal life with Him in heaven, only by continuously abiding in Christ, knowing Him more, and His laws of life.

May God bless you!
With love
Sunday Adelaja

1

THE LAWS DEFINING LIFE

God helps us in many and wonderful ways, but unfortunately, we only accept a small part of His help. This situation can be changed. If you understand the laws of life and the way they work for you, if you will constantly live by them, then you will certainly become a successful person and every day of your life will bring you joy and pleasure. This will enable you to say with confidence, that you do not just exist on earth, but you are truly living a meaningful life. The children of God are supposed to live this way because they are the ones who establish the Kingdom of our Lord Jesus Christ on earth.

PRINCIPLES OF BUILDING LIFE

Many people who live according to the customs of the world think that all the events taking place in their lives are predetermined by destiny. However, in actuality, this is not true and it does not agree with what the Bible says. This great and wise Book, the Bible, has been given to us specifically for the purpose of discovering the principles according to which life is built. Life on earth is created by God according to certain laws and principles; therefore it is predictable for those who know them and live according to them.

The Bible does not only reveal God's principles of life, but also gives many examples of how these principles worked in the lives of specific people. This means that by observing the principles of life established by God, it is possible to have predictable results and blessings in life. In the same way, the result of the life of a man who does not observe God's principles and laws is also predictable. it is possible to predict in advance or predetermine that the result would be negative.

We know that the law is good if one uses it properly.

1 Timothy 1:8

God has established laws and principles for our good, and the person who follows them devotedly will have a wonderful result in life. The Bible gives us many examples of great people who observed God's principles and consequently had results which were worthy of imitation.

These were absolutely different people. They had different character features, social status and lived in different historical times. They became history makers who influenced the destinies of many generations by observing God's principles of life. Because life is predictable, we too can have the same results and achieve what they achieved by imitating them and following the same principles by which they lived. It is not that difficult to achieve success in life if we know and understand the laws and principles of life.

Jesus Christ told His disciples that any tree can be recognized by its fruits.

> **By their fruit you will recognize them. Do people pick grapes from thorn bushes, or figs from thistles? Likewise every good tree bears good fruit, but a bad tree bears bad fruit. A good tree cannot bear bad fruit, and a bad tree cannot bear good fruit. Every tree that does not bear good fruit is cut down and thrown into the fire. Thus, by their fruit you will recognize them.**
>
> *Matthew 7:16-20*

It is possible to predict the type of fruit that a tree will bear. Pears will not grow on an apple tree, and the orange tree will not bear pineapple fruit. Our life, in the same way, is predictable. This is what Jesus was telling His disciples in the passage quoted above.

The fruits of a person's life are the results of the principles by which he lives. If the rules, laws, and principles by which a man is guided in life are known, it is possible to predict precisely what his life would look like.

KINDS OF LAWS

Life is based on the laws established by God. The person who is obedient to these laws will receive the results promised by the Lord. Unfortunately, the majority of people in this world live only by following their own assumptions; they live 'by feelings.' They only find out that they have acted incorrectly after making a mistake. Life is a continuous experiment for such people. This is a big problem of our time.

The children of God, on the other hand, have the opportunity to know the laws of life and live according to them.

We will examine the main laws that guide us in life. All the laws by which life on earth is based can be conditionally divided into several groups or categories:

- Civil laws - regulate relationships in any society. The life of any state is impossible without certain laws which regulate the behavioral norms of the citizens of the state.

- The laws of nature - regulate all natural phenomena on earth. The law of gravity, which is also known as the law of universal gravitation, for example, belongs to this category. According to this law, everything existing on earth is drawn or gravitates to it by the force of gravity and thus, it remains and is held on the surface of the earth.

- The laws of the universe or laws of life - knowing these laws is very, very important for man, however, this is the area where many are ignorant. It is impossible to have a meaningful life without knowing the laws of life. Without them, human life cannot be productive.

- Spiritual laws - these are the laws revealed to us by the Bible. Observing these (spiritual) laws does not relieve a man from complying with all the other laws mentioned above.

- The laws of success - these laws state that God has created nobody to be a loser. There are no losers from birth. God has created every one of us for success and prosperity, but without the knowledge of the laws of success, it is impossible to achieve it.

- Financial laws - it is necessary to understand that money does not go to those people who pray and fast well or to those who observe municipal or spiritual laws. Money will go only to those people who know and obey the laws of money diligently.

This means that you can be the most righteous person in your city and still not be rich. Why, because you do not know the laws which govern money.

In order to become rich, you need to study these laws and observe them. You can be the kindest person in the world, but this will never make you rich. You can die of hunger, despite your kindness, if you do not know the laws of money.

Often we feel frustrated and think - *"This person is so kind, but he is so poor! He almost doesn't have anything!"* The truth is that this person will remain poor until he comprehends the laws of money.

- Physiological laws or the laws of the body - neglecting these laws can lead a man to serious consequences that are threatening to life. For instance, the spirit will leave a body that is damaged by a terminal disease. In other words, taking appropriate care of the body to maintain it in a good condition increases the chances of a man to live longer.

THE LAWS EXALTED BY GOD

It happens very often that when we come to God, we devote a lot of time to our spiritual development neglecting all other areas of our existence. This is a big problem that many Christians make because in the course of time, when things are not working as expected in the other areas of their lives, they begin to think that God does not want to act in their lives. However, God is not to be blamed. He has created life on earth within the boundaries of certain laws. And only if we know and obey these laws, can we have a meaningful life on this earth. Even if we violate these laws without knowing, there is still a repercussion. In fact, the violation of any law carries a certain punishment with it. So, it is useless to cry out to God hoping for His help. God will do nothing.

Certainly, He can interfere supernaturally sometimes and perform a miracle. This is an exception, not the rule because He is a God of principles, a God of laws, a God of order and rules. Hence, He strictly observes all the laws and principles established by Him.

The Bible says,

It pleased the LORD for the sake of his righteousness to make his law great and glorious.

Isaiah 42:21

We can see from this Scripture that God has exalted not His name, but the law. The Bible repeatedly confirms the fact that God exalts the order (that is, the law established by Him) more than His name.

I will bow down toward your holy temple and will praise your name for your love and your faithfulness, for you have exalted above all things your name and your word.

Psalm 138:2

The word 'law' has several meanings in the Bible. It means the truth, the word, the commandment, the charter. God has exalted the law even above His name. This means that you may call upon His name repeatedly, pray and go to church on a regular basis, and He will still not change the circumstances of your life if you do not carry out certain rules which He has established.

For example, God has already established the law that He will rebuke the work of 'the devourer' if we will give tithes and offerings. If you do not carry out His word but only pray, God will do nothing. No matter how much we pray, God has already exalted His law above His name. His name will not work if we break the laws that are established by Him.

QUALITY LIFE IS A RESULT OF OBSERVING THE LAWS

Each one of us should know God's laws that govern our lives. Our lives will not be filled with various unexpected situations if we know the laws. Our lives will be predictable for us as we can foresee many events. Knowing God's principles, we ourselves can build our life the way we want to see it. Never believe that someone has already decided your destiny. That's a lie! No one has the right!

God has given us laws and rules so that being guided by them, we would live a meaningful life. If we will follow His laws, He guarantees us any good thing that exists under the sky.

The Bible gives us examples of the lives of different people who achieved success so that we, by studying and applying the laws by which those people lived, can achieve the same results in our own lives.

It is useless to argue with the perfect wisdom of God's laws because many facts confirm the infallibility of these laws. The Bible is a book of facts. It tells us about the lives of many people and this convinces us that the action of God's laws is indisputable, and it is always for the good of man.

Man cannot affect the action of these laws in any way. He should simply obey them, otherwise he will lose God's blessing. For example, king David of Israel was a man 'after God's heart,' but having violated the law by committing adultery with Bathsheba, he was consequently punished for his sin.

THE LAW IS A BLESSING, NOT A RESTRICTION

Most believers focus only on the spiritual laws. They are guided mainly by these laws, not knowing that there are many other very important laws. However, if we don't know these other laws, it would be impossible to have a meaningful life here on earth. We can predict the results of our actions in life just by knowing these laws.

Different laws influence different areas of life. A person who knows these laws can achieve success in different areas. However, more often than not, people do not like to observe the laws, thinking that they limit their freedom. Such view is simply a mistake. Observing the laws is not a restriction; it does not limit our freedom. On the contrary, it gives us an opportunity to live in all the fullness of life, enjoying it to the fullest.

The laws are not our enemy. They protect us, and obeying them, give us protection from different problems and cataclysms taking place in the world.

To the law and to the testimony! If they do not speak according to this word, they have no light of dawn.

Isaiah 8:20

God advises us to constantly focus on the law and revelation in order for us not to be guided in life by the opinion of people. God knows that observing the laws gives a man peace and rest, eliminates chaos and vanity, and establishes God's order in his life.

OBSERVING THE LAWS IS AN OPPORTUNITY TO PREDICT THE FUTURE

Life is built on certain principles, that is, laws or truths which manage this life. As it is seen from the Bible, each phrase spoken by Jesus Christ reveals a certain principle to us.

The whole word of God is a presentation of principles. That's why we need to constantly read and live by it. The

Bible shouldn't be read as a regular book. When reading the Word of God, it is necessary to always meditate upon the principles that are stated in it and also learn to apply them practically in life.

Understanding the principles by which life on earth was created gives us the opportunity to understand the truths which keep this earthly world in certain order and how to apply them in order to make our lives productive and meaningful. By observing the laws established by God, we can be sure of attaining similar results as people who applied these laws before us.

Principles and their results are always fixed. If we live by the principles of God, we can always count on a specific result. We can know in advance what to expect. That means that we can predict our future life.

Anybody can achieve the same results which someone else has already achieved before. To do so, you just need to apply in your life, the same principles by which the particular successful individual had lived.

We can repeat results by repeating principles. There are no restrictions! We just need to understand how to apply the principles that give such high results in our lives.

The only limitations that exist for us are the limitations in our mind. As soon as we unblock them by having our thoughts changed, all the barriers in our way will disappear. Then our mind will become clear, and our vision will be precise. We will be able to predict our future because we will know in advance the results of the principles by which our life is built.

It is impossible to achieve success in life without the laws. Each of us should examine our self and our life in order to understand in which areas, or in what situations we need to apply a particular law. Only then will we be able to live productively and have a meaningful life.

There are no limits in the life of those who know God's principles and live according to them. We can become the person we want to be! For this reason, each one of us must search for knowledge, the wisdom of God. We need to work persistently in order to receive worthy results and to glorify the name of Jesus Christ. In many ways we should be different from the people who live by the customs of the world, because we are privileged to know the secrets that lead to successful and happy life.

Our life can be predictable. It should be precise and purposeful, based on principles of the order of life and productivity. We should not emulate those whose lives are guided by customs, mood swings, and different assumptions and opinions.

We have enough examples of successful people whose names are forever in the history of mankind. The Bible tells us about them, revealing the principles of their lives so that by imitating them, we can have the same meaningful and quality life.

Life has been predictable for many men of God. So it should be for each one of us if we are determined not to just live it vainly, but to completely devote it to serving God and mankind, establishing here on earth the wonderful and fair laws and principles of God's Kingdom; the Kingdom which was given back to man [this earth] by Jesus Christ Himself. He expects us to continue and finish everything that has been started by Him so that the glory of God would be seen on earth as it is in heaven.

GOLDEN TRUTHS

- Life on earth was created by God according to some laid down laws and principles.
- God has established the laws and principles for our good.
- Children of God have the privilege to know the laws of life and live according to them.
- The fruits of life are the results of the principles a man follows. The violation of any law attracts a certain punishment.
- God has given us laws and rules so that by being guided by them, we would live a meaningful life.
- Principles and their results are always constant.
- It is impossible to achieve success in life without observing the laws of life.

2

RELATIONSHIP WITH GOD IS THE MAN CONDITION OF THE PREDICTABILITY OF LIFE

THE SOURCE OF LIFE IS GOD

To live a fulfilled life, a man needs to be constantly fed from his source. This source of life is God because He is the Author, Creator and founder of life on earth. The Bible says that there is no other source of life.

Jesus answered, "I am the way and the truth and the life. No one comes to the Father except through me."

John 14:6

The Lord says that He is the life, and this life is created according to certain laws and principles. So life is not an abstract and indistinct concept. Life is God. The source of life is hidden in Him, and He has given a part of it to each of us.

All the fullness of life is hidden in God; therefore, without Him it is impossible to live a whole life. It is impossible to know the laws of life without knowing its author and founder. He alone gives the breath of life.

The LORD God formed the man from the dust of the Earth and breathed into his nostrils the breath of life, and the man became a living being.

Genesis 2:7

As we see from this Scripture, God breathed life into man. Consequently, He is the source of life. The energy creating life is hidden in Him. Therefore, a true meaningful human life is impossible without God. Human life without a relationship with God is simply a mere existence.

People are in search of true life everywhere: in discos, night clubs, saunas, spas, alcohol and drugs. It is impossible to find life where it does not exist. It is impossible to find a source of life in something, created by human hands.

True life is hidden in God and you can find it only through Jesus Christ. Regardless of where a man lives and how old he is, he can only find true life with God, because relationship with Him is the main condition of a deep understanding of the laws of life and its predictability. Life can only be predictable for a man who has constant personal relationships with God, who is the author of life on earth.

THE BASIS OF LIFE

Life loses its sense without God. That is why everyone needs to know the most important law of life: *the source of life is hidden in God.* Without this source, no man on earth can live a truly fulfilled life. Great people like Abraham Lincoln, Taras Shevchenko, Leo Tolstoy, and many others, who lived before us, perfectly understood this principle. Human life without God is like a house built without a foundation. It will be unstable and will exist only for a short time. Human life without God is extremely unstable and unpredictable because the fullness and the sense of life are hidden in Him. Human life without God is similar to a small abandoned boat in the middle of an ocean storm.

In God, a man finds everything he needs: peace and rest, joy and strength, wisdom and love, stable success and riches. God reveals the laws of life to him, and God's perfect order comes to every sphere of his life. The man himself changes; this can be seen in his character, actions, and relationship with people.

A man who knows God finds stability in life. Nobody or nothing can disturb his rest because his life is brightly shining with the light of God's truth. Aspiring to please God, to glorify Him, to affirm His will, His laws and the principles of His Kingdom on earth should be the motivation of our life.

Only God can reveal to us the secrets of laws of life. The true knowledge of good and evil is hidden in God alone. Only He knows what is good and what is bad for us. Without God, people wander in darkness. They don't obey His laws, and consequently, make numerous mistakes in life that brings fatal consequences to them.

Observing the laws of God protects and preserves us. The laws become God's reliable cover (for us), making our life stable and peaceful. By His laws, God reminds us of what and when to do something because He knows our future, which is not visible to us yet.

We should communicate with God daily, because we need Him every day. We need His reminders, provision and protection. Such communication is attained through prayer, reading and meditating on the Word of God, reading Christian literature, and so on.

If we lose relationship with God and deviate from Him, then simultaneously, we begin to break His laws. In this case, numerous unsolvable problems appear in our life. However, if our communication with God is constant, we will joyously obey His laws. We will be filled with His power, anointing, energy, grace, wisdom and ideas, and we will be able to accomplish our mission here on earth.

God gives us wisdom and knowledge of His truths, laws and principles of life, so that by living according to them, we can become successful and show forth the glory of our Lord Jesus Christ on this earth.

WE WERE CREATED BY GOD TO LIVE FOR HIM

We were created by God not to simply exist on this earth and live our lives the way we want; indulging in our evil desires and lusts. God has given us life so that we would live by His principles and for Him; executing His plans and ideas. He tells us through apostle Paul:

> **Be imitators of God, therefore, as dearly loved children and live a life of love, just as Christ loved us and gave himself up for us as a fragrant offering and sacrifice to God.**
>
> *Ephesians 5:1,2*

Living for God is the highest level of life that can possibly exist on earth. This is life according to God's laws, His standards and rules. The world around us is full of temptations. The knowledge of God's Word gives us wisdom to relate soberly to life and understand that a sin leading to death is behind each temptation.

Some people wrongly think that life with God is full of restrictions and limitations; making it boring and uninteresting. However, we Christians know that by living for God, we absolutely lose nothing. It is quite the opposite! We gain a lot. We gain a true, joyful, happy and successful life because in God we obtain the knowledge of the laws of life.

Living for God is a gain. Such life is not threatened by the unpredictability. It is predictable. The people living with God and for His sake know the purpose of life and how to attain it. They know what they should do in different situations to achieve success. They also know the consequence of breaking God's laws due to their inexperience or imprudence. Living for God is protected by God and it is always meaningful.

We were created by God to be His representatives, His messengers on this planet. We were created by God to live for Him and execute His plan. He reveals the laws of life on the earth to us, and desires that we would show forth His glory here. By knowing and observing the laws of life, we will definitely bear fruits which will testify about the sovereignty, wisdom, love, riches and mercy of God to the world.

Living for God is a life that glorifies Him. God will be glorified only when we precisely follow the rules and laws established by Him for life on earth.

LIFE BY GOD'S PLAN

Life according to God's laws and plan is the true life. Being created in the image and likeness of God, we should imitate Him in everything. However, you can only imitate somebody you know well. Only if you know God personally, can you walk with Him hand in hand and closely watch Him.

It is impossible to know God and His laws, if we don't know His Word. The Word of God is a tool given to us by God to understand Him and the laws by which life operates on earth. We see how these laws work in the lives of many people. We can learn from their life experience and achieve success as they did. We can avoid the mistakes made by people who lived on the earth before us.

God's laws are firm; they do not vary with time. Therefore, by studying and deeply analyzing the lives of our ancestors, we can see the results of the laws of life, and get invaluable life experience without which a meaningful life on earth will be impossible.

To live with God and according to His laws is always beneficial, because this always brings God's blessings. Life with God and according to His laws is the only true life, which can be predicted. It's the life of success and prosperity. It's the life, which leaves a "footprint" for many future generations on earth. This is life according to God's plan.

GOLDEN TRUTHS

- It is impossible to know the laws of life without knowing its author and founder.
- Human life without a relationship with God is simply a mere existence.
- Life loses its sense without God.
- Human life without God is extremely unstable and unpredictable.
- God has given us life so that we can live according to His laws and for Him; fulfilling His plans and ideas.
- Living for God is the highest level of living.
- Living for God is protected by God and it is always meaningful.
- You can only imitate somebody you know well.
- It is impossible to know God and His laws, without knowing His Word.
- God's laws are firm; they do not vary with time.
- To live with God and according to His laws is always beneficial because it always brings God's blessings.

3 THE LAW OF CREATION

BEFORE THE CREATION OF THE WORLD...

The law of creation is also called, by some people, the law of faith. It states that all visible things emanate from the invisible. For each of us, it means that our whole life (both present and future) already existed in the spiritual world.

The Bible says that we have been chosen by God in Jesus Christ even before the beginning of the creation of the world. It means that we have already existed in the spiritual world prior to the beginning of creation of this earthly material world.

For He chose us in Him before the creation of the world...

Ephesians 1

Apostle Paul knew that everything existing in the visible world comes from the spiritual world, which is invisible to us. Things that are invisible to a man can become visible in the material world, if he firmly believes in it.

Now faith is being sure of what we hope for and certain of what we do not see.

Hebrews 11:1

This is why the law of creation is sometimes also called the law of faith. Faith is being sure of what already exists in the spiritual world.

God has certain plans and ideas for us. They are as numerous as the sand of the sea. However, the problem many people have is that they often do not know God's plans for their lives. Not knowing how to be connected to God and download this "database" into our mind, makes it impossible for us to accomplish God's purpose. We can connect with God only by faith. By this faith we can make the things that God has prepared for us, come true.

EVERYTHING WE NEED ALREADY EXISTS IN GOD

First, we need to always remember that everything we need already exists in God. Therefore, it is necessary to find God to receive what we need. However, there are certain rules to observe in order to find God and obey Him. Certain rules have to be observed before we can receive in the physical world, the invisible things from the spiritual realm.

God has many blessings for you in the spiritual realm. However, receiving those blessings depends on your knowledge of how to receive them and your willingness to observe God's rules.

Never stop at your accomplishment, never stop aspiring for new things because God has immeasurably more and greater things in stock for you. You just need to learn how to receive everything that is prepared for you by God from the spiritual realm. To do this, it is compulsory to observe the law of creation; the law of faith.

We see how this law works in the beginning of the creation of the world.

In the beginning God created the heavens and the earth. Now the earth was formless and empty, darkness was over the surface of the deep, and the Spirit of God was hovering over the waters. And God said, "Let there be light," and there was light. God saw that the light was good and He separated the light from the darkness.

Genesis 1:1-4

God already knew what He would create before He started creating all the things that exist on earth today. He would not have said "Let there be light" if He had no idea of what light was. Prior to the beginning of the process of creation, God had already known what He wanted and what He needed. He saw everything that will be created by Him.

We also need to learn to paint the picture of the plans God has in stock for us, in our imagination. This is why we need to have a vision and plans, which include the assurance of the things not seen (the unseen), but expected (hoped for).

THE ABILITY TO LOOK AT THE UNSEEN

Undoubtedly, we need to work to transfer our desire from the spiritual world into the physical world. We need to diligently work in the right direction. To accomplish this, we need to acquire certain knowledge.

Everything that we have achieved so far is already visible to all, therefore, it should not be too important to us anymore; in fact the Bible says that we need to look at the things that are still invisible.

For our light and momentary troubles are achieving for us an eternal glory that far outweighs them all. So we fix our eyes not on what is seen, but on what is unseen. For what is seen is temporary, but what is unseen is eternal.

2 Corinthians 4:17,18

All the visible things cannot be interesting to us anymore. In other words, it is not worth spending your time anymore on what you have already done. Hand it over to your secretaries, managers, or assistants, so that you can have the opportunity to look at the invisible things, and attain them. Every one of us needs to learn to see the invisible.

This is why I plant satellite churches. This is why I even handed the management of our central church "The embassy of the Blessed Kingdom of God for all nations" over to my wife. I know that I have to look not at the visible, but at what is still invisible in this world. It is better to hand over the management of what has already been built by you to someone else, so that you can move forward.

This is observing the law of creation; the law of faith. The law of faith states that there is something greater than what you have today. There is much more in the invisible world, than what we can see in the physical world now. Therefore, we should not concentrate on the visible. There is more for us in the spiritual world, than what we have already achieved on earth. There are more opportunities for us than we see in real life today. There are more chances and more resources.

However, if we are concentrated only on what we have already achieved, if we do not aim forward, that means we are not able to look at the invisible. It indicates that we do not know the law of creation. You can learn about it in more detail from my book **"Accessing divine Wisdom,"** in which I thoroughly explained how to receive answers to your needs from the invisible world.

LIVE BY FAITH

Faith is being certain of what we do not see. Therefore, we should be concentrated on the invisible, which we want to make visible. It is written in the Bible, that a righteous man will live by faith:

...The righteous will live by his faith.

Habakkuk 2:4

...The righteous will live by faith.

Romans 1:17

It means that a righteous man constantly sees and imagines the invisible things, which no one else, apart from him, sees, and which he does not possess yet. He is engaged in, and concentrates his attention particularly on the invisible things. He sees what does not exist in the visible world yet, and this is very important for him. He lives by faith in this invisible things.

If you are a righteous person, you will live in a similar way! You will live not by what you have or have attained today, but by what is known to no one else. You will see what will happen in five or ten years, and you will already start building the foundation for these invisible things to become a reality in your life!

The righteous will live by faith. Just as the righteous, we look at, and work on the invisible things only. We do not stop at what has already been achieved. We are guided by what we cannot see, by what does not exist yet in the physical world; but already lives in our imagination and thoughts. By faith we have the assurance of what we hope for, and we are fulfilling it already today.

We Christians should not remain on the same level for a long time, because our God is God of progress. Just like Him, we should be moving forward constantly, and be certain of what we do not see.

Personally, I constantly work on what is not visible to others yet; but is accessible in my thoughts and to my inner vision. I am already thinking of how I will take care of my seven children; my wife and I are planning to adopt four children. I am already putting plans together for their lives, because we have planned the lives of our own (biological) children a long time ago.

Some people think that because I think about the future, I do not see the present. The truth is that the present has been planned by me long time before it came. I do not stay on one level and concentrate only on the present. I move forward, thoroughly planning the future, which though today has not manifested yet, will surely become real (the present), tomorrow.

This is the law of creation. If you will be able to live like this, then your life will be successful because you will always accomplish those new things, which you can transfer from the invisible spiritual realm into a visible reality. You will always move forward, you will not have long pauses in life. If you lost your job, you will praise God! If you went out of business, you will praise God! No matter what happens in your life, you will always give thanks to God for everything, because you have numerous new ideas ready for implementation! You are ready to accomplish God's new plan for your life, which has been developed by you a long time ago; therefore, you will not be upset or disappointed. You will not remain on the same level for too long because you are always ready for constant advancement.

Potentially, you always have much more in the unseen world, than you do in reality. Your unexploited opportunities are hidden in God. They already exist in the spiritual realm. You just need to follow the Lord, and having discovered these invisible opportunities, start achieving them.

GOLDEN TRUTHS

- Everything existing in the visible earthly world originated from the spiritual world, which is invisible to us.
- God already knew what He would create before He created all the things existing on the earth today.
- Everything we need already exists in God.
- We have been chosen by God in Jesus Christ even before the foundation of the world.
- Every one of us needs to learn to see the invisible things.
- Potentially, you always have much more in the unseen world than you do in reality.
- We should be concentrated on the invisible things, which we want to make visible in reality.

4 | THE LAW OF TIME

LIFE IN TIME

The law of time is one of the most important laws of life on earth. The wise king Solomon, who obviously meditated upon this law a lot, came to this conclusion:

There is a time for everything, and a season for every activity under heaven: A time to be born and a time to die, a time to plant and a time to uproot, A time to kill and a time to heal, a time to tear down and a time to build, A time to weep and a time to laugh, A time to mourn and a time to dance, A time to scatter stones and a time to gather them, a time to embrace and a time to refrain, A time to search and a time to give up, a time to keep and a time to throw away, A time to tear and

a time to mend, a time to be silent and a time to speak, A time to love and a time to hate, a time for war and a time for peace.

Ecclesiastes 3:1-8

All the events on the earth happen in time. God has placed all the history of the existence of the earth in time. In other words, certain events are programmed for every time. Therefore, having an understanding of the law of time, it is possible to predict what should happen at a certain time. You can learn more about this in my book "Time is life."

THE UNDERSTANDING OF TIME IS THE UNDERSTANDING HOW LIFE FLOWS

Every person should learn to discern the seasons of time, and particularly the season he is in, at the present moment. This is necessary because there are certain life events for each time, and a man should be prepared for them in advance. Understanding the law of time gives us an understanding (which is concealed in God) of how our lives flow. All the events of this life are concealed in time. Every new time reveals new events, which have already existed in the spiritual realm. However, in order for these events to be revealed in the physical world, it is necessary to know how the law of time operates and to have an understanding of time.

The law of time is also known as the law of changes. This law states that there is nothing static in life, everything changes in it constantly. Certain changes happen in the course of time, both in the reality around us, and in each one of us. We all change with time, both on the inside and the outside because the law of time states that there is nothing constant in life on earth. Time changes events and people.

Therefore, there is no reason to be upset about your situation today, if you are not satisfied with it. Everything may change tomorrow. There is no reason to be depressed for those who know how the law of time works. There are continuous changes as a result of this law here on earth.

TIME CHANGES CIRCUMSTANCES

The law of time is also known as the law of dynamics, which states that everything is in the process of development. Everything on earth transforms from one state into another, from the worse to the better. Even after we grow old and die, we will go from a worse state to a better one, because our mortal body will be replaced by an imperishable body.

The law of time states that no matter how dark the night is - a beautiful morning will surely follow it. There will always be a bright dawn at the end of the night. For this reason, this law teaches us to hope for the best that is awaiting us in the future. It comforts us by saying, that there are no circumstances that cannot change. Maybe we don't notice these changes, but they definitely take place. Our planet earth is in motion every day. It rotates around the sun, it rotates around its own axis as well. Every moment, everything on earth is moving, and this means that it is changeable. Everything on the earth changes in the course of time.

Time passes by, and we are amazed at the things that were bothering and upsetting us yesterday. The law of time continues to be in action, and therefore, after the time of hardship, there comes a time of joy and triumph. After crying, there is always a reason to laugh. After mourning, there comes a time to sing and dance.

This law states that, our reaction to circumstances is the most important thing that determines our condition. It depends only on us whether we will be extremely disappointed with the circumstances around us, and be dominated and crushed down by them; or we will patiently wait for the time of victory over these circumstances.

The main thing is not what is happening to you in your life now, but how you react to it. Those who know the law of time, react to everything happening from a peacefulness position. They know that time changes circumstances, and therefore, they can easily go through them. The circumstances around them do not have any authority over them. According to the law of time, they are compelled to change, as they cannot exist all the time. Therefore, we can have control over them.

THE MOST PRECIOUS RESOURCE

The majority of people waste a lot of time for nothing. Here is what the wise king Solomon of Israel said:

Whatever your hand finds to do, do it with all your might, for in the grave, where you are going, there is neither working nor planning nor knowledge nor wisdom. I have seen something else under the sun: The race is

not to the swift or the battle to the strong, nor does food come to the wise or wealth to the brilliant or favor to the learned; but time and chance happen to them all.

Ecclesiastes 9:10,11

The most precious thing out of all you have on earth is time. Many people will try to take over your time. If you are insufficiently disciplined in your business, if you do not fight to spend your time on the things you have planned it for in advance, then other people will manage your time for you.

Every one of us needs to learn to protect our time, in order to spend it only on things that will draw us nearer to our set goal. If we really want to be productive and fruitful, if we want to achieve high results in life, then we need to spend our time only on the most important things, on things of highest priority.

Every one of us should learn to use time wisely and be able to manage it, in order to become the owner of our own time. There is a battle for every minute of our time in the world. Every unnecessary phone call, every unplanned meeting is an attack on your time. It is an attempt to take over your time, in order to distract you from important issues. The people distracting you probably do not even think that they are stealing your time. They are just a tool in the devil's hands. His task is to give you no opportunity to attain God's purpose on time. This is why it is so important to plan your time and protect it.

If you are undisciplined in your personal life, and you cannot say "no" to people, they will definitely take over your time, the time you have planned for very important things.

THE PRICE OF TIME IS HUMAN LIFE

The level of respect of a person to himself is defined by how much he can hold on to his plans. If a person respects himself, then he will definitely execute the things he planned. This means he can keep the promise he made to himself. If a person is careless with his plans, then he respects neither himself, nor other people. Such a person holds a very low position in the eyes of God, and He cannot entrust him with any important and responsible business.

If you do not have a specific life plan, if you do not plan your time, then it will simply fly away. You will not be able to redeem the lost time to do the things you were supposed to have done some times ago; yesterday, few days, weeks or a year ago.

Analyze your life. How much of your precious time do you spend on really important issues? What is the rest of your time spent on?

It is impossible to define the value of time. Its true price is our life. Time is given to us by God to bring forth fruit for His Kingdom and accomplish everything He has plans for our life. Do you see the results of your life, will they satisfy God? Won't chaos and idleness devour your time?

If at the end of each day, you do not have a concrete result, which you can characterize in certain figures; it means that vanity has taken a hold of your time. It is managing your life.

We should protect our time, and be focused on achieving results at all times. The achieved result is equivalent to how useful we used our time. We have to manage our time, and this means to manage our life. Do not allow circumstances or other people to manage your time. Plan your time; otherwise, it will be planned by others for you. Appreciate your time, constantly realizing, that you only have a concrete certain time period to fulfill what God has predestined for you. The life of each one of us is limited in time; therefore, we cannot afford to lose even a moment in it.

LIFE IS GIVEN ONLY ONCE

Human life is not just a record of the days a person has lived. Life is an opportunity; it is a chance that is given to a man only once. God expects us to use this time only in the best way possible, so that we will not regret an aimlessly lived life.

However, unfortunately to a great extent, the majority of people will never understand this until their lifetime comes to an end. Many of us often treat life too carelessly, not realizing that it is our only chance. We treat it as if it will never end. We live our life, as if we will live forever, and consequently, we manage it the way we want.

We should constantly analyze the way we live. Do we treat our life rightly? Do we value our life? Or are we simply wasting it? You may treat life in different ways.

It is possible to just waste time; people, lacking wisdom do so. It is even possible to ruin your time, and this is what foolish people do as well. Wise people see life as an opportunity and use it to serve. What do you personally do with your life? How do you spend your time? The majority of people, approximately about 70% of people living on the earth, spend their time thoughtlessly. They eat, go to work, sleep, give birth to children, eat, and sleep again, etc. Those who ruin their life with partying, having fun, committing adultery, drinking, and smoking etc. Are like the blind, simply going straight to hell, and not worrying about it at all.

However, those who have wisdom have understood that life is time, which must be maximized effectively. Life is an opportunity, for a short time on the earth, to secure your future in eternity. You seem to understand this especially well, when someone dear to you, or someone you knew well passes away. Then you start accessing your life in a totally different way. You try to filter your life, in order to know what you should not spend your precious time on any more, and what you should continue doing; what should be the priority of your life, and what you should not focus your attention on.

The right to manage our time at our own discretion is given to each one of us. However, we should ask ourselves this question, will we be satisfied with how we spent the time given to us, when we get to the end of our life? Are you ready to end your life right now and go to heaven? God would like you to always be ready to come to Him in heaven, not regretting anything.

For this purpose, you need to value heaven more than the earth. You need to know that you live on the earth only for the sake of pleasing heaven. If you live like that, then all your thoughts, purposes, and aspirations will be concentrated only on pleasing God and glorifying Him;

you will be ready to die for His sake at any time, knowing that you used your time to its fullest.

God has prepared everything for your life on earth to be successful and prosperous. He has prepared everything you would ever need to do in the time given to you, the things for which He gave you your life.

God's goal is to establish His Kingdom on the earth, as it is in heaven. This is His program, which we Christians, are called to fulfill. It is not a simple program. Only strong, courageous, and wise people, who have the understanding of time, and know its price, can carry out this program. Such people live purposefully. They know the purposes they want to attain in life, they know what to do, and the time they need to act. They see their future because they know that it can be predicted, if they build their life according to the laws and principles of God.

It is very important that every day of our life is spent for God, so that we would joyfully give back to Him and His works everything He has blessed us with in this life. This is why we should constantly use our time to its fullest. It is very important for every one of us to learn to see our life the way the Lord sees it and do what He desires. We should see ourselves as a part of His Kingdom; we should see ourselves as one with God. Then we will be able to use our life time - our chances and opportunities - in the right way, fulfilling God's plan on earth.

So then, each of us will give an account of himself to God.

Romans 14:12

Our life time on earth is given to us by God with a specific purpose. Therefore, we need to learn to use our time according to God's plan in order to fulfill what He has for us. There is nothing more important than this. Apostle Paul perfectly understood that the main thing in life is to attain the set goal and please God. Therefore, his life time was used to know Jesus Christ and His will.

But whatever was to my profit I now consider loss for the sake of Christ. What is more, I consider everything a loss compared to the surpassing greatness of knowing Christ Jesus my Lord, for whose sake I have lost all things. I consider them rubbish, that I may gain Christ And be found in him, not having a righteousness of my own that comes from the law, but that which is through faith in Christ - the righteousness that comes from God and is by faith. I want to know Christ and the power of his resurrection and the fellowship of sharing in his sufferings, becoming like him in his death, And so, somehow, to attain to the resurrection from the dead. Not that I have already obtained all this, or have already been made perfect, but I press on to take hold of that for which Christ Jesus took hold of me. Brothers, I do not consider myself yet to have taken hold of it. But one thing I do: Forgetting what is behind and straining toward what is ahead, I press on toward the goal to win the prize for which God has called me heavenward in Christ Jesus.

Philippians 3:7-14

Apostle Paul appreciated life, he valued his time. He knew its value and he understood that he can live his life only once, and that he will give an account of himself to God.

GOLDEN TRUTHS

- All the events on the earth happen in time. God has placed all the history of the existence of the earth in time.

- There is nothing static in life, everything in it changes constantly.

- Time changes events and people.

- There are certain life events for each time.

- Everything on earth transforms from one state into another; from the worse into a better one.

- Our lifetime on earth is given to us by God with a specific purpose.

- The main thing is not what is happening in your life, but how you are reacting to it.

- The most precious thing out of all you have on earth is time.

- Every one of us should become the owner of our time.

- The level of respect a person has for himself is determined by how much he can hold on to his plans.

- It is impossible to define the value of time. It's true price is our life.

- We have to manage our time, and this means to manage our life.

- Life is an opportunity; it is a chance that is given to a man only once.

- Life is an opportunity, for a short time on the earth, to secure your future in eternity.

5

THE LAW OF SELF-REPRODUCTION

THE POWER OF POTENTIAL

Life on earth is subject to the law of self-reproduction, which is also called the law of multiplication, or the law of potential. It states that "everything created by the Lord has the power of self-reproduction within itself."

So God created the great creatures of the sea and every living and moving thing with which the water teems, according to their kinds, and every winged bird according to its kind. And God saw that it was good. God blessed them and said, "Be fruitful and increase in number and fill the water in the seas, and let the birds increase on the earth." And there was evening, and there was morning — the fifth day. And God said, "Let

the land produce living creatures according to their kinds: livestock, creatures that move along the ground, and wild animals, each according to its kind." And it was so. God made the wild animals according to their kinds, the livestock according to their kinds, and all the creatures that move along the ground according to their kinds. And God saw that it was good.

Genesis 1:21-25

Everything that has the life of God contains the power of self-multiplication within itself. Initially, a great power to reproduce according to one's kind has been given to any of God's creation.

It is written in the Scripture quoted above, that the Lord created big fish and told them to multiply according to their kind. In other words, God created only one sample of all living things, but within each of them, He has enclosed the power (the potential) for multiplication.

The law of self-reproduction operates in all areas of human life. It says that if we do have something (even if it is small), we should not worry. The initial position is not important. The important thing for us is to know the law. We know that everything created by God has the power to multiply within itself; it has the power of self-reproduction and expansion (to spread around).

The important thing is not how you begin any business. It is important for you to understand, that everything you have today has the ability to be multiplied and become a lot bigger with time. Therefore, according to the law of self-reproduction, you need to develop what you already have, that is, to multiply it.

For example, in the beginning God created only one man. Today there are already more than six billion people living on earth. This is a result of the action of the law of self-reproduction.

Everything big begins with something small, which is capable of multiplying. Not knowing this law, many people aim for the big, and as a result they have many troubles and problems. The person who desires to have everything instantly and in large quantities is a greedy self-interested man. The Bible warns of what awaits such person.

People who want to get rich fall into temptation and a trap and into many foolish and harmful desires that plunge men into ruin and destruction.

1 Timothy 6:9

There is nothing wrong with being rich. But a man, who desires to have everything instantly, breaks God's law. He is being guided by his lust and consequently makes rash decisions, which subsequently will bring him many problems.

The law of life says that it is impossible to have everything instantly. A certain time is necessary for any multiplication, including financial one. Breaking this law, a man runs into temptation and many reckless lusts, he will imperceptibly fall into the devil's slavery. Usually, such a person cannot think and analyze deeply, and therefore he is unable to understand how God's laws work.

CONDITIONS FOR MULTIPLICATION

The law of self-reproduction states that God has put into each seed which has life in it, the ability and the power of self-reproduction and self-multiplication.

This can happen only if this seed is sown into a good and appropriate soil.

It appears that certain favorable conditions are necessary for a seed to grow and multiply. If you put the seed of any plant on a table, it would not be able to multiply there. The seed can only bring harvest if you put efforts in creating the necessary conditions for its multiplication. Otherwise, the law of self-reproduction will not work.

A man needs to discover all the abilities he has and then developed them; otherwise, they will simply be useless. It is the same in agriculture, to get a harvest from any grain, you need to go to the field, get rid of weeds, dig and prepare the soil, then plant a seed and look after it; fertilizing and watering it. It works the same way practically in every area of life.

Every talent or ability you have from God is capable of bringing you untold riches you can only dream of. You already have a potential which includes everything necessary for you to be financially successful.

Nevertheless, for you to really achieve such success, you need to develop your abilities and talents.

Every person has a potential of many abilities and talents, but not everyone makes enough efforts to discover and apply it in life. Therefore many people just live their life, not taking the advantage of the potential, which has initially been built-in in them.

It is sad to realize that this potential will be buried in a cemetery with the man who possessed it, but unfortunately, made no effort to discover it. That is why it is possible to consider any cemetery as the richest place on earth, because of the number of buried talents and abilities that the owners did not take any advantage of during their lifetime.

Unfortunately, many people will be very disappointed when they see God in heaven, if in their earthly lifetime, they do not apply maximum efforts to discover and multiply what He has initially put inside each of us.

INCUBATION TIME

According to the law of multiplication, any seed should undergo an incubation period before it becomes visible. In other words, before germination and growth, any seed stays in the soil and remains invisible for a certain time.

The Bible says that nothing was visible on earth until the moment when God began creating the earth. Only the Spirit of God was hovering over the earth. That was an incubation period. Any seed undergoes this stage before reaching maturity and bearing fruit.

This tells us that everything on earth undergoes certain stages of development. Do not expect that everything will be done instantly. Remember that God's miracles are only exceptions to the rules. Therefore, do not hope that by doing nothing, you will have everything. That is a lie and wickedness. Do not expect miracles when you should be obedient to God's laws. Do not expect God to do the things you can, and should do yourself, for you. Don't expect the harvest tomorrow if you just have only sown a seed today.

Be patient and learn to wait, because there is a waiting period for everything that will be multiplied. If you have started a business, you will have to go through a period of failures, or the time when nothing turns out. This is an incubation time. If you have invested money, then for some period of time you will have to wait until it will bring you certain income. Do not allow greediness to ruin you and your business. Do not forget, that everything sown has an incubation period.

30, 60, AND 100 FOLD

As much as God loves us, He will not give us everything instantly. Any seed can be multiplied step by step. A big forest can grow from one seed of any kind of trees, but a certain time is required for this to happen. This principle is relevant to all spheres of human life. God does not give a man everything immediately. He always gives only a small seed, and certain conditions are required for its multiplication.

As the Bible says, any seed given to us by God has the ability to be multiplied. However, this happens in different ways because a seed can bring harvest in thirty, sixty, and hundred fold. Jesus Christ spoke about this to His disciples:

That same day Jesus went out of the house and sat by the lake. Such large crowds gathered around him that he got into a boat and sat in it, while all the people stood on the

shore. Then he told them many things in parables, saying: "A farmer went out to sow his seed. As he was scattering the seed, some fell along the path, and the birds came and ate it up. Some fell on rocky places, where it did not have much soil. It sprang up quickly, because the soil was shallow. But when the sun came up, the plants were scorched, and they withered because they had no root. Other seed fell among thorns, which grew up and choked the plants. Still other seed fell on good soil, where it produced a crop—a hundred, sixty or thirty times what was sown. He who has ears, let him hear."

Matthew 13:1-9

This Scripture talks about a seed, which Jesus refers to as God's word. Many Christians often use this example, speaking about finances, although in actuality, Jesus was not talking about money here. He simply shared on a principle of self-reproduction. He taught His disciples that any seed has the potential to increase the initial result thirty, sixty, and hundred times, depending on the conditions and efforts put in by a man.

Jesus, through this parable about a seed, shows us the factors that influence the law of reproduction. First, you need to sow a seed to receive harvest. The harvest cannot come where nothing is sown.

Secondly, productivity is influenced by the type of soil. The size and quality of your harvest always depend on the kind of the soil you sow your seed in. As seen from this parable told by the Teacher, good conditions are required for a good harvest. The quality of the soil in which a seed is sown influences the end result.

Thirdly, the result is influenced by the faith of the man who sows. If he does not expect to get a good result, he will not get it. As already stated, only the things that exist in the spiritual world are revealed in the physical world. By faith, a man brings forth the harvest he is expecting in the material world. The absence of faith leads to bad harvest.

Fourthly, it is necessary to always be able to rely on God to receive a good harvest, because He is the one who grows the seed sown by us.

I planted the seed, Apollos watered it, but God made it grow. So neither he who plants nor he who waters is anything, but only God, who makes things grow.

1 Corinthians 3:6,7

So, the law of self-reproduction says the following:

- Any of God's creation has the ability within itself to multiply, that is, it has a seed;
- Any seed can be multiplied thirty, sixty, or hundred times.

MULTIPLY GOOD WORKS

God's blessing or seed can come to us in the form of an idea, thought, purpose, or some other abilities. Everything we have today can be increased or multiplied. For example, if you are a pastor of a church with 10 members, start looking at these people like at a seed. These 10 people can become a thousand, if you know God's law of self-reproduction and you are able to apply it to your life.

Everything you have today can be multiplied by God if you are obedient to His laws. If you have a hundred dollars, this can become ten thousand dollars because any seed is capable of being multiplied.

God desires that we would multiply everything He gave us. The parable about talents, told by Jesus Christ testifies to this:

> **Therefore keep watch, because you do not know the day or the hour. Again, it will be like a man going on a journey, who called his servants and entrusted his property to them. To one he gave five talents of money, to another two talents, and to another one talent, each according to his ability. Then he went on his journey. The man who had received the five talents went at once and put his money to work and gained five more. So also, the one with the two talents gained two more. But the man who had received the one talent went off, dug a hole in the ground and hid his master's money. After a long time the master of those servants returned and settled accounts with them. The man who had received the five talents brought the other five. "Master," he said, "you entrusted me with five talents. See, I have gained five more." His master replied, "Well done, good and faithful servant! You have been faithful with a few things; I will put you in charge of**

many things. Come and share your master's happiness!" The man with the two talents also came. "Master," he said, "you entrusted me with two talents; see, I have gained two more." His master replied, "Well done, good and faithful servant! You have been faithful with a few things; I will put you in charge of many things. Come and share your master's happiness!" Then the man who had received the one talent came. "Master," he said, "I knew that you are a hard man, harvesting where you have not sown and gathering where you have not scattered seed. So I was afraid and went out and hid your talent in the ground. See, here is what belongs to you." His master replied, "You wicked, lazy servant! So you knew that I harvest where I have not sown and gather where I have not scattered seed? Well then, you should have put my money on deposit with the bankers, so that when I returned I would have received it back with interest. Take the talent from him and give it to the one who has the ten talents. For everyone who has will be given more, and he will have an abundance. Whoever does not have, even what he has will be taken from him. And throw that worthless servant outside, into the darkness, where there will be weeping and gnashing of teeth.

Matthew 25:13-30

As we see, the master was dissatisfied with the servant who did not multiply what he had received. A just punishment was expected on this servant, because he had broken God's law of multiplication.

God expects that you would multiply absolutely everything you have. Do not be like the lazy slave who frustrated his master. Multiply everything that God has already given you, and you will receive much more. Tell many people about every miracle that God has done in your life, so that it will generate even more miracles. Any person healed by God can multiply God's healing if other people will find out about it. A man set free from drug addiction can bring at least 10 drug addicts to God, and they will also be set free. In such a way this person will multiply his deliverance from addiction. Everything given to you by God should be multiplied. It means that we should always apply the law of multiplication in life, in order to please our Master and glorify His name.

Some people ask me sometimes, why we pay so much attention to advertising the works that God does through our church. The reason is that in such a way, we multiply those good works which are being done by the Lord on earth. If you do not spread what God is doing, then other people would not hear and know about His mercy and grace. God says that our light should shine before all men, so that they may see our good works and praise the Heavenly father.

In the same way, let your light shine before men, that they may see your good deeds and praise your Father in heaven.

Matthew 5:16

People will not be able to see God's light in us, if it is hidden by us. They would not know about God's works, if we do not tell people about them. Therefore, we should not keep secret what God has done in our life. By testifying to the world about God's works, we can change many people's attitude to God and enable Him to work in their life.

GOLDEN TRUTHS

- Everything created by the Lord has a power of self-reproduction within itself.

- The law of self-reproduction operates in all areas of human life.

- Everything big begins with something small, which is capable of multiplying.

- A man, who desires to have everything instantly, breaks God's law.

- A certain time is necessary for any multiplication.

- Certain favorable conditions are necessary for multiplying a seed.

- Every person has the potential abilities and talents, but not everyone puts efforts to discover and apply them in life.

- Any seed should undergo an incubation period.

- Do not expect God to do for you the things you can, and should do yourself.

- The harvest cannot come where nothing is sown.

- The quality of the soil, in which a seed is sown, influences the end result.

- By faith, a man brings forth the harvest he is expecting in the material world.

- Everything you have today can be multiplied by God if you are obedient to His laws.

- Everything given to you by God should be multiplied.

6

THE LAW OF SOW-ING AND REAPING

THE PRINCIPLE OF BOOMERANG

The law of self-reproduction is very closely connected with the law of sowing and reaping. Sometimes it is called the law of seed and harvest or boomerang law. This law states that a man unavoidably reaps in his life, what he sowed because God multiplies everything by its kind.

The law of sowing and reaping states that any seed sown by us will definitely give fruits. If we sow something good, then even more good will come to our lives. Wickedness also gives its fruits. Consequently, the person who does wicked things on earth and expects something good in his life, is doing that in vain.

Our actions today will lead to our results tomorrow. What we have today is the result of our actions yesterday. Therefore, it is senseless to accuse other people of our problems. Simply, everything sown by us has brought its result; in other words, it has come back to us like a boomerang.

Truly, a man will reap what he sows. Therefore the Bible teaches us to do unto other people what we would want them to do to us. Jesus Christ was trying to teach us this law particularly, when He said that the second most important commandment is to love your neighbor as yourself. The law of sowing and reaping lies in the basis of this commandment.

This law teaches us the principles of relationships with people and the world around us. Our attitude to people determines their attitude to us. If you want people to treat you well, then you should first be kind to them. If you are harsh to people, it is unfair to expect them to be kind to you. If you sow wickedness in life, you will unavoidably reap it either directly or indirectly. The Bible says the following on this:

Do not be deceived: God cannot be mocked. A man reaps what he sows. The one who sows to please his sinful nature, from that nature will reap destruction; the one who sows to please the Spirit, from the Spirit will reap eternal life. Let us not become weary in doing good, for at the proper time we will reap a harvest if we do not give up.

Galatians 6:7-9

The law of reaping and sowing states that God gives a seed to the sower. The person who does not sow, who does nothing, is the one who does not receive anything from God.

Now he who supplies seed to the sower and bread for food will also supply and increase your store of seed and will enlarge the harvest of your righteousness.

2 Corinthians 9:10

God gives a seed to the sower. If you want to have good relationships with people, start sowing something good in them. Start sowing, and then God will give you even more seed. It is useless to demand love from people. Start loving them, and then God will fill their hearts with love to you. Do not expect someone to bless you, because God gives a seed only to the sower, who is already sowing. If you do not bless anybody with anything, then do not expect any blessings from other people. Start doing what you expect from the people around you first.

If you will sow nothing, do not expect a harvest. Whoever sows generously will always reap generously. In other words, the range and size of your blessings depend on the quantity of the seeds you sow. If you put a lot of efforts in sowing, then your harvest will be plenteous.

The law of sowing and reaping states that it is impossible to expect a big harvest from a minimum effort. It will be worthless to expect greater results if you are doing nothing with the results you have now. It is impossible to expect a promotion or increase in salary, if you only put the least required energy in performing the work you are paid for. If you put a minimum effort in your work, the payment for your effort also will be minimal.

Learn to work in such a way that requires no supervision. Do not count on any appreciation from your management. Live by God's principles, and then it will be unimportant to you whether someone sees your work or not. According to the principle of sowing and reaping, you will definitely receive what you have sown, regardless of whether people saw it or not.

It is unimportant, whether you have received any appreciation from people. What is important is that the law of sowing and reaping remains constant; therefore, all your efforts will definitely bring corresponding results.

Some people pray and expect God to do what they are asking Him for. However, they do not think, that God cannot break the principles established by Him. Therefore, no matter how much you pray, do not expect any result if you are sowing nothing. Multiplication is impossible without a seed. Harvest is impossible without sowing. If you sow nothing, God has nothing to multiply. Therefore the Bible tells us:

Give and it will be given to you. A good measure, pressed down, shaken together and running over, will be poured into your lap. For with the measure you use, it will be measured to you.

Lukas 6:38

Generous people are always generously blessed by God. Those who work diligently and honestly will always see results of their work. The law of reaping and sowing works for every person, both for Christians and non-believers. Those who observe this law will always reap a bountiful harvest of God's blessings: goodness, happiness, joy, love, wisdom, prosperity, and success.

THE SOWER OF A SEED WILL REAP FRUITS

Unfortunately, many people constantly expect that soon and very soon, a miracle will happen in their life, and that everything will change. They entertain themselves with empty illusions and hopes, and as a result, they remain in the same place for many years because nothing changes in their life.

The truth is that these people do not know the laws and principles by which life is built, and therefore they simply live by guess and by trial and error in life. One of the principles of life is that every person does not have the things he expects or dreams about, but he only has what he receives as a result of his obedience or violation of certain life principles. For example, if you want the next year to be a good and productive year for you, then you should already sow certain seeds this year to that effect. Only in this case, do you have the right to expect to have a harvest next year. If you have not done anything in this current year, and you were not obedient to certain laws of nature, then you have nothing to expect next year.

A miracle will occur only in the case, if a man will make at least one step toward God, Who will make ten steps toward him in return. Only those who act according to the laws of God can count on God's blessings.

All of us should understand that this world is based on certain principles and laws. And as already stated, God has created the earth and has established certain rules of its existence. The observance or violation of these rules determines the kind of life each of us would have. The quality of our life today is the result of how we observe the laws, which were established on earth.

Everything that you did yesterday, affects your life today. For example, if you do not like your weight today, then try to recollect when was the last time you went to the gym or at least did your morning gymnastics. If you have sown nothing yesterday, do not hope for a result today. If you do not work, do not expect to receive a salary; if you are careless with your health; then do not be surprised that sickness will overcome your body. If you break the law, it will affect your life.

The life of every one of us today is the sum total of the results of the laws, which we either obeyed or broke yesterday. The person, who knows the principles of life and observes them, has a strong foundation in life. He simply enjoys life. While, another man endures and suffers, not knowing that the reason for his sufferings is hidden in his ignorance of the laws of life.

Under equal life conditions, one person may enjoy life, while another person expresses his discontent. For example, a single girl who knows the principles of life will not be upset with her loneliness. She understands, first, that there is the other side of a coin in marriage; that marriage is hard work and sacrifice, and she is not quite ready for it yet. Therefore, she patiently waits for her time, preparing herself for future matrimonial life. Being single does not bother her, because she is occupied with certain businesses all of her time. She reads books about marriage and child training, she consults with married women, learning from their marital experience, she goes to clubs for singles. She sows now in order to reap in the right time.

The girl, who does not know the laws and principles, will definitely be suffering from the fact that she is still not married, while her peers have been married for a long time. She is only distressed about her status, but she does nothing to change the situation. She sows nothing; therefore, it is pointless for her to expect a result. She will not be able to be happy in marriage, because she had sown nothing into it.

Many Christians frequently live by illusions. They think that attending church gives them a right for a successful life. They are seriously misguided, because attending church can only help them to learn about the laws by which life is built. However, observing these laws depends on them only.

If you want your life to change in a specific area, then you need to start sowing into this area, that is, start doing something concrete in this direction. Then the Lord will show His might and power, and you will see what He is capable of doing.

GIVING

Giving is sowing everything you have into the lives of other people. You can sow your time, knowledge, talents, finances, etc in them. The Bible says that giving makes us happy people.

In everything I did, I showed you that by this kind of hard work we must help the weak, remembering the words the Lord Jesus himself said: "It is more blessed to give than to receive."

Acts 20:35

It is more blessed to give than to receive. Giving actually is an investment, which brings a certain profit. It is much more blessed to give because you have already sown and in time of your need or crisis, you can be assured that God will not leave you.

If you were blessed today - it is good, but there is no guarantee, that you can receive something tomorrow as well. However, if you are the one not being blessed, but the one, who blesses, then by doing so, you are taking care of your future, because in case of any need, God will definitely come to your aid and will fulfill your needs according to His riches.

And my God will meet all your needs according to his glorious riches in Christ Jesus.

Philippians 4:19

Become a constant sower, and then you will be a blessed man. Everything sown by you is being gathered in heaven into a cup of blessings, which having overflown, will plentifully pour over you, just like the rain pours on the ground. Therefore, it is not worth worrying, if God's blessings are not seen in your life, in spite of the fact that you are constantly sowing. The law of sowing and reaping continues to operate, and one day you will become a witness of how God's blessings plentifully and generously pour over you.

Do not cease to sow! Do not close the heavens over yourself; otherwise you may perish in drought on this earth. Be generous in giving, multiply all the good you have - and God will increase everything you serve other people with many times.

DO NOT EXPECT APPRECIATION FROM PEOPLE

Some people complain that they have helped many people and did good things for them, but for some reason, nobody came to their aid during their own difficult times. In other words, they think that people are ungrateful; therefore, it is senseless to do good for them.

Such a position confirms the fact that very often, when we do good things, we start thinking that the people we have helped are our debtors. Therefore, we expect appreciation and good relationship from them, as a response to the good we have done.

However, God desires that we would expect nothing in return when we do good works. It is true that many people are ungrateful, but God knows how to thank you. The person, who knows the laws of life, will not wait for appreciation from the person he helped. He does not expect appreciation from people when doing good things for them. He knows that the law exists and operates; therefore, God will make it so, that other people will treat him the way he has treated somebody else.

For example, a businessman deceived his fellow countrymen and became rich. Later, he started doing business with foreigners. He expected a considerable expansion of his business because of these new connections, but it turned out that those foreigners were also deceivers, just like him. As a result of the law, this businessman became bankrupt. Boomerang has worked. What this person has sown has been returned to him.

Everything we do does not disappear anywhere. God sees everything. He rewards each person for his acts, both good and bad. Life on earth is given to us, so that we would do good things to people, give them joy and inspiration. Our calling is to make people happy. Therefore, we cannot be indifferent to the grief, depression, and sadness that are still around us.

We are the representatives of God's Kingdom, and our task is to fill this earth with joy, love, and peace. We have to do good things on this earth and help people become happy.

That is why many members of our church take part in various church activities. They desire to serve people, that is, to do good things for them. By doing so, they serve not just specific people, but they also serve God and believe that He will bless them.

Do not be deceived: God cannot be mocked. A man reaps what he sows. The one who sows to please his sinful nature, from that nature will reap destruction; the one who sows to please the Spirit, from the Spirit will reap eternal life.

Galatians 6:7,8

You cannot sow into God and be in a losing position. You cannot work for God and reap nothing! You will definitely see the results: happy faces of saved people, joyful families, the youth who have been set free from addiction and have received prospective goals and direction in life.

God rewards man for everything. That is why it is worth doing good works for people; it is worth sowing love on earth, because God will eventually return it into our life and the life of our descendants.

IT IS ALWAYS BENEFICIAL TO DO GOOD

No matter how your life turns out, or what trials and difficulties you had to go through, you should never let your heart get hardened. It is senseless to repay evil with evil, because in this way, the evil is increased even more. Evil can only be overcome by good; therefore, it is always beneficial to do good works. This is what God's word teaches.

Now a priest of Midian had seven daughters, and they came to draw water and fill the troughs to water their father's flock. Some shepherds came along and drove them away, but Moses got up and came to their rescue and watered their flock. When the girls returned to Reuel their father, he asked them, "Why have you returned so early today?" They answered, "An Egyptian rescued us from the shepherds. He even drew water for us and watered the flock." "And where is he?" He asked his daughters. "Why did you leave him? Invite him to have something to eat." Moses agreed to stay with the man, who gave his daughter Zipporah to Moses in marriage.

Exodus 2:16-21

This Scripture records the act of Moses, who defended Reuel's daughters from the shepherds. This act resulted in Moses finding a roof over his head in a foreign country, and later, he got a wife. This is how the law of sowing and reaping operates. It is always beneficial to do good to other people, as it brings God's blessings into our lives.

Certainly, it was not easy for Moses to protect the girls. It was possible that his own situation was a lot worse than the situation of those he defended. Imagine that Moses, who was raised up in the luxury of the Egyptian Pharaoh's wealth, suddenly found himself in a desperate situation: no money, no food, no place to live, and no protection. In addition, Pharaoh's servants could have been searching for him, to punish him for murdering an Egyptian.

However, in this difficult situation, Moses was not complaining about life. He was not thinking of his own problems - rather he solved the problems of other people who needed his help. When he was in need, he did something good to other people - and God rewarded him for it. This way, another of God's law - the law of rewarding worked.

Practically, Moses was in the position of a homeless person. How often some people, including Christians, look at homeless people with contempt, not thinking that possibly there is a deliverer and savior of people among them, just like it happened with Moses many years ago. That is why we should treat every person with respect, no matter what his position is today.

The person who is able to respect the dignity of others is worthy of all respect. All of us are created in God's image and likeness, and God respects and loves us all. We should imitate Him, and be like Him.

That is why, despite the circumstances around every one of us, we should learn to do good to people. It simply has to become our way of life. If we will do it with all of our heart, God will give us numerous pleasant surprises. The gesture of good works which we do for other people can become a solution for our problems and troubles.

It happened like that with Moses. The help he rendered to the girls, he did not know, and which is so unusual for modern men, became the means of solving many of his problems. The girls did not help Moses in any way. Probably, they even forgot to thank him. However, the Lord could not forget that. Therefore He opened the heart of the girls' father toward Moses, and he invited Moses into his house.

Moses was not upset with the girls for not reacting in the best way to his kind act. He also did not expect any appreciation from them, perfectly understanding their uncomfortable condition. He just blessed (helped) them and left in peace. This tells us that when doing good things for other people, we should not expect anything in return from them. In most cases (about 90%), we will receive the reward from an absolutely different source.

Do not expect anything in return when doing good works. Simply do good things for people for the sake of God. Let God Himself reward you, and let Him give it to you whenever He thinks it is necessary. If you want to receive God's reward, then do not expect any appreciation from people. Do good - and immediately forget about it! Close your eyes to it. Do good and do not expect any reward for it. Do good things on earth with joy.

No good work, which is done with a pure conscience, will go unrewarded. As already stated, if you do not expect a reward from people, then you can receive a higher reward. The wise apostle Paul knew the law of sowing and reaping very well, and thus spoke:

Let us not become weary in doing good, for at the proper time we will reap a harvest if we do not give up.

Galatians 6:9

When doing good things for people, you will not always receive the reward right away. Usually, doing good requires consistency. Continue doing good works, even if nobody notices it. Continue doing good works, even if you face persecution, humiliation, and insults as a result. Do not react to the response of other people to your good works. Just continue doing it. Continue doing good works, remembering that God is testing you. I doubt that He will reward somebody, who only once in a lifetime has done something good for someone. That could only be an exception. God will definitely examine the motive of your good work. He desires to know, for what or whose sake are you doing the good work - is it for the sake of receiving a reward or because you want to imitate Jesus Christ?

Probably, some people will not understand why we do good things. They will condemn us and speak negatively about us. Very often because of this, some believers stop doing the good works, God has called them to do. More often, a person stops doing good just before the breakthrough; just before God's blessing. Therefore, God warns us in the Bible that the rewarding time will definitely come, if we have enough patience to wait for the time appointed by God.

Let us not become weary in doing good, for at the proper time we will reap a harvest if we do not give up.

Galatians 6:9

Doing good always brings a harvest, it cultivates good fruits. However, it is necessary to remember that a certain time should pass from blossoming to gathering fruits. Therefore, do not give disappointment and depression any place in your life. Do not allow your problems to close your eyes to the needs of other people, do not become self-centered. Do good deeds to people!

SOW GOOD WORK INTO THIS WORLD

Everything that you do in relation to other people will be done by people in relation to you. If you do good to people, then God will encourage other people to do good to you. If you deceive, steal, and betray people, then God will find a way for someone to do the same to you.

So in everything, do to others what you would have them do to you, for this sums up the Law and the Prophets.

Matthew 7:12

The essence of the Gospel is hidden in this Scripture. God wants us not just to talk about love, but to act in love. The people will treat you the same way you treat them. God always returns to you what you do to others. This is the law of sowing and reaping in action. It is also called boomerang law.

God has created the world in such a way that our attitude to other people would be reflected in their attitude to us. The people who live by the norms of the world, know nothing about this law, and consequently, have many problems and troubles in life. God allows His children to know how to act in the right way to avoid many problems. That is why He has given us His Word - to reveal the laws of life to us.

Do not be deceived: God cannot be mocked. A man reaps what he sows. The one who sows to please his sinful nature, from that nature will reap destruction; the one who sows to please the Spirit, from the Spirit will reap eternal life. Let us not become weary in doing good, for at the proper time we will reap a harvest if we do not give up. Therefore, as we have opportunity, let us do good to all people, especially to those who belong to the family of believers.

Galatians 6:7-10

It is necessary for every one of us to analyze and investigate our life; what is it filled with? What are we sowing into this world? How do we treat the people around us? We need to remember, that all of this will come back as a boomerang to us. God Himself will repay us for what we do to other people. Therefore, no matter how people treat us, we should do good to them. The seeds sown by us will definitely be multiplied, and after some time will return into our life again. That is why it is beneficial to do good to people. That is why it is beneficial to give them joy and happiness. By doing so, we multiply everything that we have in order to then reap a huge harvest of good fruits in our lives.

God gives us all a chance to sow good deeds into this world, for good works to fill this earth continually, by coming back into our lives. God's blessing for us is hidden in the people we do good to. By doing good works, we unlock our blessings from the Lord in the spiritual world, and put into action, the law of sowing and reaping.

GOLDEN TRUTHS

- Any seed will definitely give shoots.
- Our actions today lead to our results tomorrow.
- Our attitude to people determines their attitude to us.
- The range and quantity of your blessings depend on the range of your sowing.
- Multiplication is impossible without a seed. Harvest is impossible without sowing.
- The person, who knows the principles of life and observes them, has a strong foundation in life.
- Giving makes us happy people.
- God desires that when we do good works, we would expect nothing in return.
- Our calling is to make people happy.
- Evil is overcome only by good.
- It is always beneficial to do good to other people, as it brings God's blessings into our life.
- The person who is able to respect the dignity of others is worthy of every respect.
- No good action, which is done with a pure conscience, will go unrewarded.
- Good always brings a harvest, it cultivates good fruits.

7

THE LAW OF CAUSE AND EFFECT

A RESULT IS IMPOSSIBLE WITHOUT AN ACTION

There are certain laws that govern our lives. These laws relate to different spheres of life. If you want to achieve success in a concrete sphere of life, then you need to know the laws operating in that sphere.

It is impossible to get a result without an action. In other words, if there is no action, there will be no result. Therefore, if you want to have a certain result in some sphere of your life, you need to start acting in that direction.

For example, if you want to have a good financial result, you should know how the laws of money (financial laws) operate. Without them you will not be successful in the area of finances, even if you pray about it for several hours a day. You will not be able to achieve a good financial result, if you do not obey the laws and the principles at work in the sphere of finances.

It is not enough to just know the laws established by God. You need to apply them in life. Only then, can these laws bring a real result to you. Everything you know will not give you any benefit, unless you start acting according to the knowledge you have. Action, not knowledge brings result. In other words, any action consequently causes another action, that is, a certain result.

Any object remains constant until it is changed by an external influence. In the same way, any situation in your life will remain constant, if you do not take some actions to change it. For example, if you live with a husband; an unbeliever, who is committing adultery, and you do nothing to change the situation, but just pray, then nothing will change in your life, unless you start taking some actions.

Everything remains in its previous or original condition, unless some actions are taken, or certain efforts are applied. Perhaps, you have been praying for financial breakthrough for a long time already, but in spite of the fact that you go to church, you still do not have the money you need. You will not have the money, until you start learning about the laws and principles of how money works, until you start working, and learning to invest money in the right way.

Everything in your life will remain constant, unless you start changing something in it. In other words, you need to do something to have any result. The changes toward a better life will not occur by themselves, unless you put certain efforts to it.

ACTIONS LEAD TO CHANGES

As stated already, God has placed the laws above His name; it means, that He Himself submits to these laws. Not only has God established certain laws, but He acts according to them.

Because of this, I would like to get your attention to a very educational Bible story.

> **Now there were four men with leprosy at the entrance of the city gate. They said to each other, "Why stay here until we die? If we say, we will go into the city – the famine is there, and we will die. And if we stay here, we will die. So let's go over to the camp of the Arameans and surrender. If they spare us, we live; if they kill us, then we die." At dusk they got up and went to the camp of the Arameans. When they reached the edge of the camp, not a man was there.**
>
> *2 Kings 7:3-5*

The men with leprosy, referred to in this Scripture, were Israelites. They believed in God. Just like all Israelites, they prayed to God to set their people free from their enemy. The only difference was that the other Jews remained in their houses and did nothing. They prayed for delivery, but did nothing about it, expecting that God would deliver them supernaturally (without them doing their own part).

However, God cannot break the laws which He has established. He Himself always observes these laws. One of these laws is the law of cause and effect. It states that nothing happens in life unless certain efforts are applied to make it happen. Nothing in this world happens by itself. No changes can occur without certain actions. It is a law; a constant principle our earthly world exists by.

The Israelites prayed and fasted, while they were surrounded by the Arameans. Wishing to get rid of their enemies, the Jews appealed to God. However, none of them realized that nothing would change in their destiny, until someone among them will start doing something, because God cannot violate His law.

The Israelites appealed to God but remained inactive. They knew that they had to ask God to receive what they desired. However, they had no idea at all, that there are laws of life which should be observed to receive God's blessing. Indeed, God never blesses those who break the law. The Israelis were super spiritual people, just like many contemporary Christians, who only pray, but do not want to do anything.

God, as always, was original. He found simple people, rejected by the Israeli society; it was much easier for Him to reach their hearts. God found men with leprosy outside the camp of the religious Jews. Those lepers had come to understand His principle and the law of creation. They realized that nothing can happen on its own, regardless of how much a man may pray.

We can pray, fast, proclaim, and thank God for everything, but unless we start doing something; nothing will happen. God will not act in our life if we do not act ourselves.

The lepers realized that if they, as well as all the others did nothing, they would simply die. Only when they started taking certain actions, did God's supernatural power produce miracles. God made a strong sound from their movement, and the Arameans thought that another army had come to help Israel.

> **For the Lord had caused the Arameans to hear the sound of chariots and horses and a great army, so that they said to one another, "Look, the king of Israel has hired the Hittite and Egyptian kings to attack us!" So they got up and fled in the dusk and abandoned their tents and their horses and donkeys. They left the camp as it was and ran for their lives. The men who had leprosy reached the edge of the camp and entered one of the tents. They ate and drank, and carried away silver, gold and clothes, and went off and hid them. They returned and entered another tent and took some things from it and hid them also. Then they said to each other, "We're not doing right. This is a day of good news and we are keeping it to ourselves. If we wait until daylight, punishment will overtake us. Let's go at once and report this to the royal palace."**

> *2 Kings 7:6-9*

The lepers then went to report about all that happened to the royal gatekeepers; and when the Israelites finally went out of the city and entered the camp of Arameans, they received the answer to their prayers. The enemy's camp was empty, and the Israelites took all the stocks in the enemy's camp.

Then the people went out and plundered the camp of the Arameans. So a seah of flour sold for a shekel, and two seahs of barley sold for a shekel, as the LORD had said.

2 Kings 7:16

As an answer to the Israelites' prayers, God gave them grace, and they did not have to work hard to receive clothes, meals, and riches. However, they needed to start doing something to get it. This is how the law of a cause and effect operates.

God always answers our prayers. Nevertheless, everything mentioned above testifies that only our actions generate concrete results. Only action brings a necessary solution to a particular problem. The answer to our current problem will come through prayer, but the solution to that problem will come only through our concrete actions.

As this story in the Bible mentioned above testifies, God had already heard the prayers of the Israelites a very long time ago, but thank God, He found four lepers, who decided to take action. Otherwise, nothing would have changed in the destiny of the people who were in the surrounded city.

THE KINGDOM OF GOD NEEDS PEOPLE OF ACTION

The efforts we apply cause certain changes in this world. For this reason, God's Kingdom needs people of action as one of the laws of this Kingdom says that it is impossible to get a result, if we do nothing. The Bible says:

Therefore I tell you that the kingdom of God will be taken away from you and given to a people who will produce its fruit.

Matthew 21:43

According to this Scripture, a man who does nothing is not worthy to be in the Kingdom of God, because he breaks the law of this Kingdom.

God's Kingdom is the place for people who desire to work actively and fruitfully for its good. Every Christian has to put in maximum efforts to remain in it, because God will take away not just blessings from an inactive person, but also the Kingdom itself.

As we see, it is not enough to just enter and be in the Kingdom of God. Being in it, it is necessary to work actively in order to serve in spreading the Kingdom, because that is the purpose of our God's calling.

Many people, who do not know the laws of life, calm down and rest on their laurels, when they come into God's Kingdom. They totally forget that there is a definite purpose for their salvation and calling. If they do nothing for the Kingdom, they become useless for God. In other words, an inactive person is useless for God's Kingdom.

God reveals the laws of life to His children, so that they can be useful for the fulfillment of His plan. Christians are allowed to know the secrets of the Kingdom of Heaven, so that by using them, we have an advantage over the people who live by the customs of the world and know nothing about God's laws. God gives us everything so that we would be the head, not the tail. However, if we are inactive (even if we know the laws of life), the Lord will take away everything we have from us.

> **He replied, "The knowledge of the secrets of the kingdom of heaven has been given to you, but not to them. Whoever has will be given more, and he will have an abundance. Whoever does not have, even what he has will be taken from him."**
>
> *Matthew 13:11,12*

If, knowing the laws, we start working actively toward them, then, God promises to bless us even more and multiply our fruits. That is why we should not be afraid of something new and unknown. It is known that the best way to overcome fear is to start doing what you are afraid of.

FAITH LEADS TO ACTION

Very often believers just dream to attain their goals, but do nothing about it. They talk about great results, which some day, they will achieve, but nothing happens in their life. Nothing changes in it, as they still do nothing to achieve the desired results. These people will never attain their goal, as one of the laws of life says, that it is impossible to have a result without an action.

God desires that we would have good results in this life, that is, we would bring forth fruit. We are being evaluated both by people and God according to these fruits. Revelations and dreams are not fruits yet; they are only plans which need to be carried out by acting. Without action, it is impossible to receive a result.

According to the Bible, faith always causes an action, as it is written:

Now faith is being sure of what we hope for and certain of what we do not see.

Hebrews 11:1

Having assurance is an action. To take action means to practice the laws which are revealed to us by God. The Bible says that we can be happy in this life, only if we observe the laws established by God.

Now that you know these things, you will be blessed if you do them.

John 13:17

All of Jesus' sermons teach that it is not enough to have knowledge. The important thing is observing what we know because one action is better than a thousand intentions. All our intentions are meaningless, if we do nothing toward carrying them out. There will be no result without an action; therefore our intentions will remain just intentions. They will never turn into a real business without our proactive actions.

DOERS ARE THE ONLY ONES WHO HAVE FRUITS

Very often, believers justify their inactivity by the fact that they pray and are waiting for answers from God. Sometimes, people simply "hide" behind a prayer; similar spiritual excuses have become an actual problem today. We all need to understand that prayer, faith, and prophecies do not release us from acting. Prophecies and prayers are being fulfilled, and faith becomes a real power only when we start taking actions. The law works this way. If we do not put any efforts, then no prophecy will be fulfilled, and all our prayers will remain without an answer. Our faith is dead without concrete works.

It is impossible to receive fruits without taking an action. The Bible confirms it by saying:

When you enter the land and plant any kind of fruit tree, regard its fruit as forbidden. For three years you are to consider it forbidden; it must not be eaten. In the fourth year all its fruit will be holy, an offering of praise to the LORD. But in the fifth year you may eat its fruit. In this way your harvest will be increased. I am the LORD your God.

Leviticus 19:23-25

It is very necessary to work to receive fruits. Not only must you enter the Promised land (though this is not easy because it has already been populated by aggressive and hostile people), but you need to prepare and cultivate the land. It is necessary to cultivate this land for some time, for it to become fertile. You need to get the seeds that will subsequently grow into trees. Possibly, you will need to go and find them, and then you plant them and constantly look after them, patiently expecting the time when they will start bringing forth fruits.

As this Scripture says, the fruits which can be used for food will come only in the fifth year. That is, for five years, you need to be putting certain efforts to get the fruits. All this time, you need to be doing something for these fruits to be, and for them to be ripened on time. As we see, it is impossible to receive fruits without actions. A result is impossible without an action.

Prayer without actions is also fruitless. When Moses cried out to God for the people of Israel, God answered him:

Then the LORD said to Moses, "Why are you crying out to me? Tell the Israelites to move on."

Exodus 14:15

Frequently, laziness forces us to search for easy ways, but only what is earned by our efforts brings blessings and fulfillment. The law, to which the life on earth subjects to, works in a similar way. Therefore, every one of us should work putting in all efforts to bring a powerful and long-lasting result.

He who works his land will have abundant food, but the one who chases fantasies will have his fill of poverty.

Proverbs 28:19

My friends, do not hope to receive any result, if you are not taking any action. Stop thinking that God will suddenly change your life, and by a wave of the magic wand, success will come to you. This kind of thinking belongs to parasites and needy people. Probably this statement might appear rude and strict, but it is true. That is the law established by God.

There will be no result if an effort is not applied. When receiving a blessing from someone, we should respond with mutual appreciation. It is much better to do it through ministry, showing mutual care and attention, instead of just saying a "dry" thank you. Only laziness causes someone to take, giving nothing in exchange.

Some people live, dreaming of blessings, and hoping that the Lord will suddenly open heavens, and things will become reasonable on their own. We dream, prophesy and believe; and at the same time, someone else goes, works, and receives a good result. Stop dreaming only; start creating, start doing something specific - and then God's power and grace for achieving results will be released. God honors and blesses people of action beyond their expectations.

So, here are the truths which should be known by those who want to achieve good results in life:

- God's Kingdom is intended for people who want to work actively and fruitfully for its good;

- Only what is zealously achieved with our efforts will bring blessings and fruits in life;

- God and people will evaluate our life's results based, not on our revelations, prophecies, or plans, but on our concrete actions and fruits;

- To achieve results in life, it is necessary not only to dream, but to start doing and creating something. One action is better than ten thousand intentions.

For a deeper study of this topic I recommend you to seriously meditate on my books: "How to overcome your laziness, Leader in action, Saved, and what follows, fulfill your calling, Time to dream and achieve your dreams, Who are you in history, and Spearheading national transformation."

IT IS MORE, THAN WE IMAGINE

God promised us that He will do much more for us than what we can possibly dream about.

Now to him who is able to do immeasurably more than all we ask or imagine...

Ephesians 3:20

What does this Scripture mean? What is God telling us here? Often we think, that God Himself will do more than we imagine in our wildest imaginations and dreams. This is an illusion.

God will do more than what you can do, by achieving your dream. If you will do everything you can to attain your goal, if you will use everything that is within your strengths and your opportunities, then God Himself will do everything that is inaccessible to you or is not within your strength. He will give you a supernatural power and grace to complete everything that you could never do by yourself.

However, take a closer look: He will only do what you cannot even imagine doing. He will do only what you could not have done by yourself. In addition to this, God will do all of this only in one case: if you have already done your part. If you have already actively worked on building your business, then your prayer will connect you to the source of supernatural power and opportunities. Then you will be able to do much more than you could have done on your own.

If you have done everything you could, being faithful in small things as much as possible, then God will give you supernatural opportunities to do much more. It is against His rules and laws to do for you what you can do yourself. No faith, prophecies, fasts, or prayers will force God to do for you, the things that are within the range of your opportunities. He will more likely rebuke you, than help you. Until you have done what is within your limits, you are simply as good as a wicked and lazy servant, Jesus Christ referred to this in a parable to His disciples.

Therefore keep watch, because you do not know the day or the hour. Again, it will be like a man going on a journey, who called his servants and entrusted his property to them. To one he gave five talents of money, to another two talents, and to another one talent, each according to his ability. Then he went on his journey. The man who had received the five talents went at once and put his money to work and gained five more. So also, the one with the two talents gained two more. But the man who had received the one talent went off, dug a hole in the ground and hid his master's money. After a long time the master of those servants returned and settled accounts with them. The man who had received the five talents brought the other five. "Master," he said, "you entrusted me with five talents. See, I have gained five more." His master replied, "Well done, good and faithful servant! You have been faithful with a few things; I will put you in charge of

many things. Come and share your master's happiness!" The man with the two talents also came. "Master," he said, "you entrusted me with two talents; see, I have gained two more." His master replied, "Well done, good and faithful servant! You have been faithful with a few things; I will put you in charge of many things. Come and share your master's happiness!" Then the man who had received the one talent came. "Master," he said, "I knew that you are a hard man, harvesting where you have not sown and gathering where you have not scattered seed. So I was afraid and went out and hid your talent in the ground. See, here is what belongs to you." His master replied, "You wicked, lazy servant! So you knew that I harvest where I have not sown and gather where I have not scattered seed? Well then, you should have put my money on deposit with the bankers, so that when I returned I would have received it back with interest. Take the talent from him and give it to the one who has the ten talents. For everyone who has will be given more, and he will have an abundance. Whoever does not have, even what he has will be taken from him. And throw that worthless servant outside, into the darkness, where there will be weeping and gnashing of teeth."

Matthew 25:13-30

As we see, God is calling us to be awake, that is, to take action. Thus, only those who take action, get results. We can call those who take action "doers." The Lord is in such a great need of them. That is why He thanks those servants who are obedient to His laws. They do not just sit there with their arms folded, doing nothing; but they work persistently, multiplying the good works of His Kingdom.

The principle of God is clear. He glorifies and exalts only those who are obedient to Him; obedient to the rules of life which are established by Him. That is why He lifts up those who persistently put efforts in order to achieve something other people would not even attempt. The more complicated the problem to be solved is, the more you will be able to discover your opportunities and abilities as you solve the problem. Step by step, moving forward in overcoming the difficulties, a man will be able to discover his maximum potential and achieve the highest results. The more efforts he puts in, the higher his productivity will be. One of the laws of life on earth works in such way.

ACT IN ORDER TO GIVE GOD AN OPPORTUNITY TO ACT

God is capable of doing a lot on this earth; but He will not begin to act, if we would not start taking actions. Today many Christians know that God has a destiny for everyone He has chosen. God has a purpose for our lives, but it will never be fulfilled, if we do not start taking actions actively. Communication with God should not be a "one-way traffic." We have to allow God to speak to us when we are communicating with Him. We should have the time, which we dedicate to listening to what He wants to say to each one of us.

We should apply everything we hear from God, in life. Every idea, which we receive from Him, should be implemented. Otherwise, our life will remain the same, no matter how much we pray for change. Nothing will change in it, unless we start taking actions.

Personally, I try to start taking actions immediately, after receiving another revelation from God. This is not that easy, because every person is prone to slothfulness, inertness, and sometimes simple laziness. I aim to start bringing God's envisioned plan to life, immediately. Though slowly, but surely, I try to move forward toward my set goal. I take actions to enable God to take actions, and to show forth His grace in my life.

I become crazy for the sake of Christ in order to fulfill what He reveals to me. I become a fanatic (a freak, in a good sense of the word) in order to fulfill God's commandment, and do what the Lord wants as soon as possible.

For example, as soon as God told me one night to open "Club 1000" (the club for 1000 Christians-millionaires living in Ukraine), I had already started distributing the application forms, the following day, to those who would like to join this club. That same day, I had done such a huge amount of work that about 200 people immediately expressed their desire to become members of this club.

We need to learn to respond immediately to God's call. This has to become a good habit for every one of us. We should develop a habit to listen to God and imme-diately show our obedience to Him. Only in such cases will we be useful for God on earth. Only in this way will we be able to fulfill His will precisely, and give Him an opportunity to establish God's Kingdom on earth through each one of us.

GOLDEN TRUTHS

- It is impossible to get a result without an action.
- God will not act in our life if we do not take action ourselves.
- The efforts put in by us cause certain changes in this world.
- A man who does nothing is not worthy to be in the Kingdom of God.
- An action, not knowledge, brings result.
- The best way to overcome fear is to start doing what you are afraid of.
- Revelations and dreams are not fruits yet; they are only plans, which need to be implemented.
- Faith always leads to action.
- To take an action means to practice the laws, which are revealed to us by God.
- It is impossible to receive fruits without taking an action.
- A prayer without actions is fruitless.
- Laziness forces us to search for easy ways.
- Communication with God should not be a "one-way traffic."
- The more difficult a problem to be solved is, the more you will be able to discover your opportunities and abilities when you start solving it.
- God honors and blesses people of action beyond their expectations.

8

THE PRINCIPLES OF A SUCCESSFUL LIFE

THE INITIAL DESIRE TOWARD SUCCESS

Every person living on this earth has an unbeatable desire to live better. Everybody wants to achieve something greater than what they have today. This need, desire, and aspiration, are a part of the expression of God's nature which is initially integrated into every person. It is said that the aspiration to grow is a natural need of every person.

A constant aspiration to be greater is God's quality in us because God is God of progress. He constantly moves forward. So if God is in us, then we also experience this internal aspiration toward advancing. Thus, God wants to be expressed through us.

...For it is God who works in you to will and to act according to his good purpose.

Philippians 2:13

Every time we have a desire to achieve something better, testifies to the fact that God's nature is being revealed in us. For example, a person may want to learn to play the piano. Why does he have such desire? It is because God initiates this desire in him. God wants to listen to His creation giving Him praise and glory; therefore, He gives him the desire to play for Him.

God lives inside of you. He is being revealed in every cell of your body, in your genes, in your bodies, in your blood. When you desire something positive - this is God, wanting to be expressed and revealed through you; He is sending you signals that He wants to do good works, to create something wonderful through your hands. He is a marvelous God - an absolute embodiment of harmony and perfection. This is why He wants His creation to reflect His perfect qualities. This is why God compels every one of us to aim for the best, to aim to achieve success.

Regardless of what the people around you would say, be guided not by their opinion, but by those wonderful desires which the Lord awakens in you. Through them, He is telling you that His abilities, reserves, and opportunities are hidden inside you. His divine energy is concentrated within you. If He reminds you of the necessity to move forward, it means that you are capable of completing the plan.

If God puts a desire into your heart, it means that His power will support this desire. His mighty power will carry out what He has planned, if you will obediently act according to His will. You just need to believe that through you, God wants to create something beautiful on earth. Here on earth, He works only through people who trust and follow Him. He searches for people through whom He can carry out all His programs, dreams, and purposes.

The main thing necessary for this is for you to start taking actions. Only those people who do something, using their abilities, talents, finances, and material property, and are willing to give even their lives for the achievement of God's plan, get to keep both their lives and what they have in it.

Everything you have should work for blessing people, and then all of it will work for your blessing. Success comes only when we multiply ourselves, our resources, opportunities, talents, and possessions. Your life should progress in everything and facilitate the progress of other people. All the resources you have are given to you so that you can serve people with them. What is not multiplied by you will be taken away from you. What you do not use to minister to people will eventually be lost by you. This is why the rich are getting richer, and the poor poorer.

May your life be concentrated on constant growth; then you will have good results in life. Growth consists of constantly overcoming problems or obstacles. The more problems a person manages to overcome, the more he grows. The more problems we solve successfully, the higher we are lifted. Everyone dreams of living a successful life. However, some people live in such a way that there is no worth from their life. Such people are more often, a burden for their relatives and the people around them. They are not living, but simply exist. Fortunately and thanks to God, there are other kinds of people on earth, whose lives are a blessing for others. Their lives are celebrated not only on earth, but in heaven as well.

Does anybody have a reason to celebrate your life? Is heaven rejoicing that you are alive? God has intended the human life to be a reason for joy both on earth and in heaven. He desires that every day spent by us here on earth will be a source of life, enrichment, and joy for the whole world. Now, how do we live this life so that it would enrich the earth and heaven? What is necessary for us to do to become a joy for the world around us? Well, we need to know the basic keys to a successful life, that is, we need to understand its basic truths, principles, and laws.

All great people, whose names are written in the history of mankind, knew these truths. If we, just like them, consistently build and create our life based on these principles, then we will definitely leave a mark in the sands of time and in life on this earth.

LIFE IS AN OPPORTUNITY TO SERVE

The first principle is this: life is an opportunity to serve. Life is given to every person, solely for this purpose. But unfortunately, very few people realize this. Sometimes, a man needs to live his whole life to fully understand this principle.

God's children have an advantage over others because the Bible reveals the secrets of the laws and principles of life to them. Christians know that the earthly life is given to them "for lease" for a short time, as an opportunity to serve God and mankind. Life is a chance, it is an opportunity. We need to invest it into other people. Only in this way does it make sense.

The person, who is living only for satisfying his own interests, lives only for himself. He is useless for the human society. Such a person becomes a slave of his own desires and ego. He is like a closed vessel from which it is impossible to get a drink; therefore, there is no worth from it.

An ego-centered person, concentrated only on himself. He always complains about life and constantly shows his discontent with everything. Things are always not enough for him; he is disappointed, and does not see any reason for joy in this life. The problem of this person is that he does not know the first principle of a successful life. He breaks this principle by concentrating on himself, and consequently, this leads to problems in his life. Self-pity, anger, rage, envy, and irritation become constant partners of people, who break the principle of serving people.

People who constantly complain about their life have not realized that this life is not given to them for the satisfaction of their whims. If a person becomes self-centered in his life, it is possible to predict (confidently) the results of his life. His life will not be successful, even if he becomes a millionaire or a president. Such a life cannot be successful because life is not given to a man to live it for his own purpose, but to serve others.

Everything that is given by God to each one of us has only one purpose: to serve God and people. If you have a talent, it is given to you to serve others. Otherwise, it is simply useless. If you are given the ability to be a teacher, what is the point in it if you do not want to teach anybody? If you have the ability to earn money, what is the point in it if you do not share it with anybody? Regardless of whatever you have in your possession, it becomes useless, if you do not use it to minister to other people.

Life is a ministry. All great people were able to achieve success in their life because they understood this law. That is why they became great; because they realized that their money, time, and opportunities are not their property, but God's trust. They are only managers of what is entrusted to them by God. Their life itself is God's trust.

We are not the owners of everything we have in this earthly life. Even our own life does not belong to us. Everything that fills this earth belongs to God.

The earth is the LORD's, and everything in it, the world, and all who live in it;

Psalm 24:1

Everything belongs to God both on earth and in heaven. He has appointed you to manage everything you use today. However, you are not the owner, because everything belongs to Him. If you have an understanding of this, you will not feel sorry for yourself. It is not your life, but God's; therefore, you need to fulfill His will. It is necessary for you to complete what He has given you this life for.

So, if a man lives only for himself, his life will be full of problems, illnesses, unhappiness, fear, and anxiety. Greatness, success, riches come to a man only when he understands, that he is supposed to live for the sake of others. For example, do you know why such great companies like Coca Cola, Procter&Gamble, McDonald's, and Pepsi Cola became so successful in the world's market? The answer is very simple. They serve a large number of people. If Coca Cola Company produced their drink only for members of their family, the world would not have heard about this company. If McDonald's cooked food only for themselves, nobody in the world would have heard about McDonald's. These and others similar companies have attained worldwide popularity because they use the principle of service, the principle of love toward people. They desire to serve as many people as possible, and this has made them popular and successful. This is a principle of life. The more you serve others, the more God exalts you.

Sometimes we think that ministry consists only of singing, praying, and teaching. In reality, God expects concrete practical actions from us in ministering to people. I think you remember very well, the story about the Samaritan mentioned in the Bible.

"What is written in the Law?" he replied. "How do you read it?" He answered: "Love the Lord your God with all your heart and with all your soul and with all your strength and with all your mind; and, Love your neighbor as yourself." "You have answered correctly," Jesus replied. "Do this and you will live." But he wanted to justify himself, so he asked Jesus, "And who is my neighbor?" In reply Jesus said: " man was going down from Jerusalem to Jericho, when he fell

into the hands of robbers. They stripped him of his clothes, beat him and went away, leaving him half dead. A priest happened to be going down the same road, and when he saw the man, he passed by on the other side. So too, a Levite, when he came to the place and saw him, passed by on the other side. But a Samaritan, as he traveled, came where the man was; and when he saw him, he took pity on him. He went to him and bandaged his wounds, pouring on oil and wine. Then he put the man on his own donkey, took him to an inn and took care of him. The next day he took out two silver coins and gave them to the innkeeper. "Look after him," he said, "and when I return, I will reimburse you for any extra expense you may have." "Which of these three do you think was a neighbor to the man who fell into the hands of robbers?" The expert in the law replied, "The one who had mercy on him." Jesus told him, "Go and do likewise."

Luke 10:26-37

Jesus Christ told his disciples what it meant to love your neighbor. As we see, a priest, and then a Levite passed by the poor man who got into trouble. Obviously, they were going to serve God, leaving the person who was extremely in need of their help, to die. These so-called ministers were going to do ministry, not taking advantage of an opportunity to provide true ministry. God had given them a real opportunity to show love to a neighbor, but they just passed by. They were in a hurry to serve somewhere else, in another place. This is a paradox!

Very often many of us, not knowing the principles of a successful life, act in a similar way. We become so religious that helping people to solve their problems is not perceived by us as a ministry any more. For some reason, there is a certain stereotype in our consciousness, and consequently, we perceive ministry only as attending church.

We have to learn to serve people the way God wants it to be done. We have to show God's love to people through our ministry to them. It is impossible to love God, and not serve people. Our prayers, in which we ask about something for ourselves, are not proof of our love to God. We will not be able to prove our love to God by the fact that we read the Bible or sing in a church choir. The only proof of our love to God is ministering to people. Only this proof is acceptable by Him.

LIFE IS RELATIONSHIPS

The second truth is this: life is relationships. Nobody can live in this world on his own. A successful life is impossible without relationships with other people. A man who has bad relationships with everybody will most likely die of depression. His job is not a joy to him, because he is arguing with everybody in his place of work. He cannot go outside, because he will find a reason for arguments there too. His relatives, neighbors, friends, and government irritate him. He judges everybody, and is dissatisfied with everything. Such a person cannot have a successful life, because life is relationships.

The more successful relationships you manage to build with people, the higher you will be raised by God. You will be a respected person in society, if you learn to establish good and fruitful relationships with people.

Nobody can be successful on his own. Success in life depends on how well we manage to build normal relationships with each other. If you are moved by love in relationships with people, it will make you great and successful.

Love is the main commandment of God, and it is impossible without relationships. The skill to build healthy relationships with people is a principle of a successful life. A man cannot be successful if he does not have healthy relationships with people around him.

HIGHLIGHTS OF RELATIONSHIPS WITH PEOPLE

What can help us create these relationships? This question is answered in the Bible:

But the fruit of the Spirit is love, joy, peace, patience, kindness, goodness, faithfulness, gentleness and self-control.

Galatians 5:22,23

First, creating relationships with people is impossible without loving them. Love is the basis of truly reliable and strong relationships.

Secondly, joy helps to create it as well. If your life is filled with joy, if your face shines, then believe me, you will simply draw people to yourself. Fellowship with somebody who constantly complains, and is in depression is uninteresting to people. They can be drawn only by your joy.

This is why God gives us the fruits of the spirit. He knows that they will help us to be successful in life. We will not have to impose ourselves on people. The fruits of the spirit shown in us will draw people to us, and fellowship with them will help us to be successful.

Thirdly, the peace your heart is filled with helps in creating relationships with people. If people see that you are able to react calmly, without irritation and anger, but absolutely calmly with everything, it will definitely draw them to you.

Fourthly, your patience and the skill to forgive will help you build relationships with people. Regardless of how people treat you, continue to show love and patience toward them. This will win their hearts and draw them to you, so that you can build good relationships with them.

Kindness, goodness, faithfulness, gentleness, self-control - each of these fruits of the spirit is a highlight; a "pearl" of relationships, which draws people to you, and helps you in building relationships with them.

THREE TYPES OF RELATIONSHIPS

All relationships with people can be conditionally divided into three groups or types.

- Relationships with people from whom we learn. Every man should have relationships with people, who are more successful in life than him. They are the people he respects and from whom he receives a rich life experience.

Each person should have such people in his life. Therefore, each one of us should find the people we can learn from, the people we would want to imitate and follow.

- Relationships with people who are equal to us. Certainly, we need relationships with people who can encourage us, who we can feel equal with, who we can relax with, feel comfortable with, and share our joys and successes with. We need people, with whom we can be ourselves, who would accept us for who we are. These are relationships with relatives, relationships with fellow workers, relationships with true friends and supporters.

- Relationships with people who follow us, the people we teach. Such relationships definitely need to be in our life. Every one of us needs relationships with people we would set an example for; people, who would like to imitate us. If you do not have the people you teach, support, and inspire, that means your life is not enriching anybody. In that case, your life is barely useful to people, and consequently, you will not be able to achieve success in it.

All these three types of relationships are highly necessary to every one of us, because they create the fullness of life and are a crucial condition for success.

LIFE IS A RESPONSIBILITY

The third principle of a successful life is the understanding that life is a responsibility.

Only those people who take responsibility for this life become successful and great in life. People who take responsibility for themselves, for relatives, and for the whole society become leaders. Those who have realized that life is a responsibility will always have followers and disciples, because these people have leadership qualities.

Have you realized this truth? Do you take responsibility? It is known that the sphere of a person's influence depends on the measure of his responsibility. What is the sphere of your influence in this world? Do you have an influence on the people around you? And what kind of influence is it? The following is needed for your influence to be positive, instead of negative:

- To serve what is good, not evil; to serve what develops, and not what destroys others.
- To have the right, pure motivation.
- To take the right actions.

People will not follow you just because you speak good and right words. These words need to correspond with your actions. If your actions testify of your godliness and righteousness, then they will definitely become a worthy example for emulation for those who are intending to follow you.

People will not follow you also if they realize that you have some motives, based on self-interest. Only your pure intentions will draw people to you.

You need to show a worthy character, have pure motivation and take right actions, if you want people to follow you. Without this, it is impossible to inspire people to follow anyone. All great people understood this. Jesus Christ gave His life to save mankind. Jesus is a worthy example for every one of us. If we want to have the same great and successful life, we need to live the same way He did, that is, we need to give all of our life to serve mankind and God.

Jesus Christ understood that life is an opportunity to serve people; life is relationships with people; life is a responsibility for the destiny of mankind. He lived His short life confirming these truths. That is why His name was exalted by the Heavenly father.

> **Who, being in very nature God, did not consider equality with God something to be grasped, But made himself nothing, taking the very nature of a servant, being made in human likeness. And being found in appearance as a man, he humbled himself and became obedient to death - even death on a cross! Therefore God exalted him to the highest place and gave him the name that is above every name.**

Philippians 2:6-9

Jesus Christ took responsibility for all mankind, therefore now the whole world is following Him.

So, here are the principles of successful life:

- Life is an opportunity to serve;
- Life is relationships;
- Life is a responsibility.

ANY SUCCESS BEGINS WITH FAILURE

It often happens that when aiming for success, a person starts a business and immediately fails. It appears that it is natural, and therefore, it is useful for us because any law works for our good. When you first look at it seems that failure would not benefit you, but real life only confirms that failure could be beneficial.

- If our business begins with failure, then later down the road we will be able to adequately appreciate the success that we will achieve with God's help.

- A man who is not afraid of failure is the only one who can become successful. The devil always tries to steal and destroy the success and prosperity of God's children, as he comes only **"to steal, to kill and to destroy"** *(John 10:10)*. The devil hates success; therefore, he attacks any successful person. The truth is that because of the fear of failure, the majority of people today are in slavery, instead of being winners. Many people having great potential are afraid to fail, and therefore, do not even try to change anything in their gray life. These people simply do not know the principles of success.

- Failure is a step to success. It would seem that Jesus Christ's death could be considered as the greatest failure in the history of mankind. The Son of God had come to earth to help people, but as a result, He was killed by them. To a naive person, this would seem like the greatest defeat in the world, the biggest failure; but the greatest victory in the history of mankind was born from this defeat.

Whatever failure would happen on your way, it is a signal that the greatest victory is awaiting you. If you have experienced a failure in the beginning of your business, that means, thank God, you were on the right track. You do not have a reason to be upset, what happened is that one of the laws of success has worked in your life. Your failure is a normal course of events. If the law is observed, it means you are on the way to success, on the way to God's blessings.

- Any failure is an excellent lesson, from which you can learn for your future. A proverb says that only an unwise or a silly man can fall into the same hole twice. Failures teach us a lot. And it is good, as we think at times, that we already know everything; and that could cause pride and superiority.

- Failures teach us not to give up, they teach us to be winners. Indeed, the winner is not the person who never loses, but the one who never gives up. As the Bible says, a righteous man will fall seven times, but he will rise up anyway. Failure forces a man to pull himself together, to pay more attention, and to be more responsible.

- Failure is not the most terrible thing that can happen in your life. Not starting to do anything or abandoning what you have started is worse than failure.

- Success is achieved by those who are ready to take risk and fail. The readiness to take risk and responsibility brings honor and respect to a man. Those who do not have the eagerness and impetus to continue moving forward, after the failure they had gone through, will never attain success.

- God can entrust success only to a man, to whom He can entrust with defeat and failure as well. The fact that you have tried to do something and failed raises you above others, if despite all that has happened to you, you will still continue doing the business you planned.

Each of us needs to learn to look at failure in another way; to look at it through God's eyes. In every failure, there is an opportunity of coming victory; we just need to show patience, courage, and persistence in achieving the purpose.

Any success is born out of failure, so, failure can be called a womb of success. Certainly, we should not constantly dwell on our failures. We have to bury their memory. Very often, the memories of past failures are so strong that they stop a person and deny him the opportunity to move forward.

Failure is a temporary phenomenon; it does not indicate an absolute defeat, but only forces you to search for other ways of achieving the purpose. Such attitude toward failures differentiates winners, or those who irrefutably attain success.

IMAGINATION IS BETTER THAN KNOWLEDGE

It is impossible to achieve success in any sphere of life if you do not know the principles working in that sphere. Christians often think that it is enough to just pray to God to have success. Not denying the importance of prayer in our life, I would like us to notice, that prayer alone is not enough to achieve success. Not to mention that in most cases, the prayers of some Christians are only their monologue, and not a dialogue (conversation) with God.

Let us take a look at how prophet Habakkuk communicated with the Lord.

I will stand at my watch and station myself on the ramparts; I will look to see what he will say to me, and what answer I am to give to this complaint.

Habakkuk 2:1

As we see, the prophet asks God a question and expects an answer from Him. In this Scripture, there is one very important lesson for every one of us. If we pray, it is important to not simply speak or ask for something. It is necessary to learn to correctly ask questions in prayer.

The second lesson we can learn in the words of prophet Habakkuk is that, it is even more important to hear God's answer in prayer. In other words, prayer is not just some conversation; it is questions and answers, a live dialogue with the individual.

It is impossible to achieve success in life without the help of the One Who is the author of life. A successful person is able to listen to the voice of the Spirit, or in other words, to his own intuition. Such person is always full of ideas. So what is an idea? We know that an idea is a tip from the Spirit. Successful people are successful because they have learned to be connected with the Spirit. Such people get exalted in life; they become great.

So, there are two secrets; two principles, which will unavoidably lead a man to success. The first one is to pray to God until you hear His answer. The second one is this: having received God's insight, use all your strength, all your energy, knowledge, and abilities to accomplish it. That was what prophet Habakkuk understood. He says: "I ask God a question, and not only do I ask, but I stand at my watch." Habakkuk did not just ask God a question; he was on guard, expecting an answer.

This is a very important principle of creating a successful life. It is important to build your life not just on the Word of God, but on the voice of God. Do everything possible to hear the voice of God, only then will you achieve everything. Any creative person will tell you, that all of their achievements became possible only thanks to inspiration. When inspiration comes, everything goes smoothly. It testifies that these people have learned to be guided by the Spirit.

The main thing for success is new ideas. The author of any new idea is God. The basis of the word "inspiration" is the word "Spirit," that is, the breath of God, which becomes a word for us. However, some people are very lazy to execute the ideas given to them by the Lord. They do not even want to try remembering them. If you really want to become a successful person, you need to make a decision to become a fan of executing God's every idea. If you are not faithful in little, God will not entrust you with greater things.

If you are not ready to work, putting your maximum effort into carrying out any idea which will be given to you by God, then you better give up any hope of becoming successful in this life.

In order to carry out an idea accurately, just like the Lord has said, it is necessary to write it down. Prophet Habakkuk calls our attention to this.

Then the LORD replied: "Write down the revelation and make it plain on tablets so that a herald may run with it."

Habakkuk 2:2

If God speaks to you about something, if He gives you a revelation concerning your life, it is very important to write it down. The revelations that are not written down can be easily forgotten, some important details may be missed in it, despite the good memory of the person it is addressed to. Many ideas from God, given to different people, remain unfulfilled and even forgotten due to this reason. Typical human carelessness and laziness are often the trivial reason for it.

God said to Habakkuk: "Write down the revelation," that is, what the prophet has seen. God wants us to learn to see. It is a required condition for any person wishing to achieve success. You will be able to write down only what you have seen. Every man has a spiritual sight, that is, inner vision, but not everyone uses it. I would like you to notice, that our inner sight is much stronger than our physical sight, but we unfortunately, rarely use it.

What is the purpose of our inner sight? Why is it given to us by God? Using our inner sight, we can create, that is, transfer to the real visible world, existing things from the invisible spiritual world. Inner eyes are given to us so that we can bring the future into the present, so that we can see, draw, and complete it. This is why God desires that we would develop our inner sight. Whoever has learned to use it will not be lacking in ideas. Whoever is able to see the future will control his life and this world.

GOOD PREPARATION IS BETTER THAN HOPING FOR A MIRACLE

Many people including Christians, for some reason think that on one wonderful day, there will be a miracle and their life will suddenly and completely change and they will become successful. This kind of mentality is simply naive because success demands constant, intense work, and good preparation. Good preparation is better than hoping for a miracle, because such hope is simply a self-deception.

Preparation is what determines who will be successful, and who will fail in life. A wise person once said a phrase that expresses the essence of achieving success: "Life rewards only prepared people." High places, positions, ranks, and awards are waiting only for those who have been diligently preparing for them. Without preparation, a man cannot reach heights because it requires a certain skill and professionalism.

Life rewards only those who are well prepared for it. Often people live by some illusive hopes, thinking that the time will come, and everything will somehow turn out well by itself. These people simply waste their precious time; the time that they could have been spending on preparation. In addition, in the future, they could attain certain success according to the level of their preparation. They should finally take responsibility for their life and start doing something tangible in achieving their purpose.

If we start getting ready, if we start changing something, creating something, then we can hope that God will come out to meet us. If we do our part, God will not be slow to do His. It is never late to begin preparation toward success, instead of wasting time on complaints. If you take responsibility for your destiny and start doing something, God will open the windows of heaven for you.

God will not work for us; He will only begin helping us if we start taking action. If you want to become rich, then start getting ready for it. Study the laws of money, the principles, and rules of investment. Get a certain financial knowledge, and the knowledge of the laws of the country where you live. If you want to have a family, start getting knowledge about family life, raising the children, making family bud get and taking care of the home. Begin with preparation, instead of hoping for a miracle, because life rewards only those who are prepared.

It is impossible to achieve success in life, relying on luck. True success involves concrete, effortful, and diligent work. Do you want to be lucky? Start creating something. Luck comes only to those who do something tangible. It never favors the lazy, and those who do nothing.

Work constantly, and raise your standards higher. Long for the new heights and reach them. Then without a doubt, you will be lucky in life, because you will become the source of your luck.

Whatever your hand finds to do, do it with all your might, for in the grave, where you are

going, there is neither working nor planning nor knowledge nor wisdom. I have seen something else under the sun: The race is not to the swift or the battle to the strong, nor does food come to the wise or wealth to the brilliant or favor to the learned; but time and chance happen to them all.

Ecclesiastes 9:10,11

As we see, the most important thing for success is time and chance, which are given by God. However, notice this: if the person is not quick enough in his business, the chance will never be presented to him. The person who does not run at all will not become a successful runner. The person, who does not fight the battle, will never win. Before time and chance will come, a man has to do everything he possibly can. If he does all that is possible on his side, then there will be a chance on his path; a chance that will bring him success.

If a man has maximum preparation, he will be most productive. Everything that your hand can do - just do it! Do not get comfortable until you have done everything the best way possible. Do not give up until you have the victory. Be persistent in your desire to achieve success, and then a chance will definitely be given to you.

So, the breakthrough in life is given only to those who persistently work. Success comes only to those, who force themselves to do what is necessary, instead of what is desirable. Only the person, who is well prepared, and can discipline himself, can count on having success, in order to not follow the flesh but to be guided by the instructions of the Spirit. Do not expect compensation without preparation, and a miracle without an effort. Work before God, work in private; and God, seeing you in private, will raise you up publicly, so that you could achieve success in this life and fulfill His plan.

SUCCESS IS ACCESSIBLE TO EVERYONE

Success is possible in all spheres of human life: in politics, business, and ministry. Success is accessible to each person. Each person can have it if only he wants it. It is not that difficult to achieve success. All that is needed for it is to know the principles of success and to observe them strictly.

So, what are the ways to achieve success? They are very important and at the same time absolutely simple ways, which can make any person successful.

Here is the first way to achieve success. The fastest way to achieve success is to answer or respond to the needs of people around you. Find problems that need a solution, and offer different ways of solving these problems.

Often people search for money to become successful. They search for success, profit, riches - and as a result have nothing, because they search for the wrong thing. You do not need to search for money: search for problems and solve them. It will lead you to success.

The fastest way to success is to help people solve their problems. Perhaps you may think that it is a waste of time because people are ungrateful? Well, do not even expect appreciation from those you have helped. God will find a way of thanking you. He has many different ways to do that. If you constantly search for an opportunity to solve people's problems, God will raise you up and bless you.

What you do for others, God will do for you. This is a golden rule of success.

The second way of achieving success is: do not search for easy ways to success because it will cause you to lose. The person who searches for easy ways always gets into the devil's slavery.

For example, some girls wishing to get rich fast, marry rich men, and then become their slaves, without any right to say anything. The fate of those who, in pursuit of "easy money," trade with their bodies is even worse. The person who is looking for easy ways will never be lucky in life.

Do not search for what is easily achievable. Always face the challenges of life with joy. The more difficult the problems you solve, the higher you will be lifted, the stronger you will become, the bigger and more stable will your success be. Search for the complicated tasks that require extraordinary solutions. Then you will always be able to easily solve problems.

If you learn to carry out difficult tasks, everything will turn out fine in your life. It will not be a difficult thing for you to achieve success, if you have learned to always train yourself. Obtaining the skill to solve difficult questions and problems will give you a good training for life.

Easy ways and easy works relax and weaken a man. However, doing difficult work will always train him. It will not be difficult for those people, who are used to doing difficult and quality work to achieve success.

The third way of achieving success is to know: Life gives us certain opportunities every day. It is necessary for us to learn to distinguish these opportunities. Every meeting, every telephone conversation, is another God given opportunity, which can become a step to success. We just need to learn to see what is hidden behind every event of our life, which probably seems absolutely insignificant to us.

Only wise and smart people see opportunities in every single day. If someone called you this day, then there is a reason why God allowed that. Do not perceive all the events of your life superficially. Look deeper, search for the original purpose the Lord has put in them. Probably, the person who called you needs help. Or, maybe this person can help you with something.

Learn to ask yourself and people the right questions. Start finding the opportunities hidden behind every acquaintance, or telephone conversation. What does God want to teach or tell you? How does He want to use this or that event of your life? What does He want to do through you today?

God has not created any day empty or insignificant. Just like the postal parcel – there is something "packed" in every day of your life. However, the majority of people never unpack their "parcels of life." This tells us that these people do not have the skills to constantly think deep, explore, and discover new things. You have to understand that every day is a parcel from God for you.

The fourth way of achieving success is: Success is often hidden in what a person does not want to do at all. The difference between successful people and losers is indeed in the fact that, successful people do not just do what they want, but what is necessary, even if they do not like it at all.

For example, not all people want to go to work every day, get up early in the morning, or stay awake at night.

However, successful people understand that success is often hidden in what is inconvenient for the flesh. Therefore, they do not live under its dictation. They are guided by the spirit in their lives, against the desires of the flesh. In fact, the Bible teaches us:

So I say, live by the Spirit, and you will not gratify the desires of the sinful nature. For the sinful nature desires what is contrary to the Spirit, and the Spirit what is contrary to the sinful nature. They are in conflict with each other, so that you do not do what you want.

Galatians 5:16,17

This Scripture reveals the fourth way of achieving success. The person, who desires to achieve it, should live under the guidance of the spirit, instead of gratifying the desires of the flesh. The majority of people in the world are used to doing what is convenient for them. Successful people force themselves to do what is needed to achieve success, but uncomfortable for their flesh.

The flesh should not govern your life; you have to learn to control it. You should always be in control of situations in your life. You cannot allow yourself to become a slave of your flesh, gratifying the desires of the flesh is a formula of failure. The formula of success is to learn to do what you do not have the desire to do.

The fifth way of achieving success is: Success is possible only for those people who work a lot and persistently; success is for those who like to work diligently. They are the people who can work smartly and effectively. Certainly, you should not become a slave of work. You have to have priorities in your life so that it is versatile and gives you the opportunity to develop as an individual, to communicate with friends, and serve other people etc.

The life of every man is not created for failures. People become losers only because they do not know how to become successful. Such people do not have the necessary knowledge; they do not have the information, which can lead to success. Also, people cannot become successful if they do not want to do something concrete toward achieving success.

Start to work, in order to find the necessary information and to fulfill it - then you will definitely become a successful person because success is possible for everyone. It is accessible and close to each one of us.

GOLDEN TRUTHS

- Life is an opportunity to serve.
- All the resources you have are given to you so that you could serve people with them.
- The only proof of our love to God is ministering to people.
- Successful life is impossible without relationships with other people.
- The fruits of the spirit in us will draw people to us.
- Only those people who take responsibility for this life become successful and great in life.
- Failure is a temporary phenomenon.
- A man who is not afraid of failure is the only one who can become successful.
- Failure is a step to success.
- The winner is not the person who never loses, but the one who never gives up.
- It is impossible to achieve success in life without the help of the One Who is the author of life.
- The main thing for success is new ideas.
- Revelations not written down can be easily forgotten.
- Good preparation is better than hoping for a miracle.
- Life awards only those who are well prepared for it.

- It is never late to begin preparation toward success.
- Breakthrough in life is given only to those who work persistently.
- The fastest way to success is to help people solve their problems.
- What you do for others, God will do for you.
- People become losers only because they do not know how to become successful.

9
LAWS OF FINANCIAL PROSPERITY

GIVE TO GOD WHAT BELONGS TO HIM

As mentioned earlier, certain laws exist in all spheres of human life. This also applies to the sphere of finance. Often, many Christians think that it is enough to pray, and give tithes and offerings to have financial prosperity.

However, we see, in real life, that not only those who give tithes and offerings have financial prosperity. Undoubtedly, those who do not give God what belongs to Him, withhold His blessings from themselves. However, giving tithes and offerings alone is not enough for financial prosperity. Although many preachers say that giving tithes and offerings brings financial blessing to us, but in reality, this is not enough. It is necessary to know certain financial laws to have financial prosperity.

Then what does giving tithes and offerings give us? The Bible says:

> **"Will a man rob God? Yet you rob me. But you ask, "How do we rob you?" In tithes and offerings. You are under a curse - the whole nation of you - because you are robbing me. Bring the whole tithe into the storehouse, that there may be food in my house. Test me in this," says the LORD Almighty, "and see if I will not throw open the floodgates of heaven and pour out so much blessing that you will not have room enough for it. I will prevent pests from devouring your crops, and the vines in your fields will not cast their fruit," says the LORD Almighty. "Then all the nations will call you blessed, for yours will be a delightful land," says the LORD Almighty.**

Malachi 3:8-12

This Scripture states that our giving, that is, tithes and offerings, testifies about our obedience to God's law, which gives Him a right to bless us.

- Giving opens a way for financial blessings, because breaking the law of tithe and offering places a man's life under a curse.
- Giving forbids the works of the devourer, that is, certain spiritual forces that destroy our finances and everything we own.
- Giving allows God to give us strength to get wealth *(see: Deuteronomy 8:18)*.

- Heaven is always opened over us, if we are faithful in giving. This means that many new ideas, supernatural opportunities and resources become available to us.

It is evident that financial prosperity is impossible without giving. However, giving tithes and offerings is not the only factor in achieving financial success. You should work hard to have financial prosperity, that is, you need to cultivate your land. This was the first task that God gave to man in the garden of Eden.

The LORD God took the man and put him in the Garden of Eden to work it and take care of it.

Genesis 2:15

Giving is a spiritual law. However, living in the physical world, we should also observe other laws, that is, the laws of the physical world. Otherwise, God will not be able to give us the blessings, which have already been reserved for us.

LIFE ABUNDANTLY

The land to till in the scripture above is a prototype of our calling, talents and abilities. To cultivate the land means to develop your gifts, in order to raise the level of what you are doing. The person who does not cultivate his land will never become rich, he will not have financial freedom. Therefore, if you have a talent, develop and improve it, then it will become one of the sources of your financial prosperity and financial abundance.

A land needs to be cultivated before seeds can be sown into it, and later have a harvest. The result of what we do in our life (the harvest of our life) should be visible. If God's blessing is not visible in our life, then we should find out the reason for this.

Some people think that if they give tithes and offerings, then they do not have to work, because the Lord Himself, having promised them an abundant life, will provide for them. Such people need to know, that if they do not produce anything, they should not expect to receive anything from God.

There is no money printing in the spiritual world; so, consequently, God will not give it to you. Money is on earth; therefore, you should put certain efforts to gain it. If you are not doing any work, not producing any goods or services, not selling or exchanging one product for another one, then where is the money going to come from?

Many believers think that the more offerings they give, the more God will bless them. However, money exists under its laws. Not only do we need to be able to earn it, but we must also be able to multiply it. Many believers are afraid to leave a comfort and familiar zone and begin something new. They have no desire to raise their educational level and learn the laws of money. However, without this, they will never be able to become financially independent.

Jesus Christ told His disciples, that He has come to give us life abundantly. He meant abundance in all spheres of our life, including finances. However, in order for us to have this abundance, we have to be obedient to the laws of life, including the laws of money. Therefore, every one of us has to know the following:

- The kindness of a man does not make him financially rich. Kindness has no relation to riches. The person who sows good will always have good relationships with other people. However, this does not mean at all, that he will have a lot of money. If a kind man does not learn the laws of money, his financial situation will not be the best.

- A man's spirituality does not make him rich. Spirituality alone is not enough to make one rich. You need to have knowledge on how to manage money properly, and to multiply it. You need to become a professional in the field of finances, because only this can guarantee you the growth of your financial well-being.

- If a man's income consists only of his wages, he will not become rich. The fact that a person has a job does not mean that he will be rich, even if it is a very lucrative job.

- To be a businessman does not mean to be rich. Today there are many businessmen in the world, but there are a very limited number of millionaires among them, because only a man, who knows the laws of money, can become rich and become a millionaire.

- The person who is simply lucky in this life cannot become rich. When riches come to a man unexpectedly, he loses them very quickly. Such sudden riches can come in the form of an inheritance or a big prize. However, not knowing the laws of money, such a man does not know how to properly manage the acquired wealth; and therefore, he loses it easily.

It would be wrong to think that our calling guarantees us financial abundance. Life testifies that very often non-believers, wicked, and mean people become rich. This confirms the fact that money does not choose only kind and highly spiritual people. Money does not choose only those who go to church. It goes to those who know and comply with the laws of money.

MONEY SHOULD SERVE US

Many Christians wrongly consider that it is improper for believers to speak about money. However, the Word of God teaches us a lot about managing finances. God has established the laws in all spheres of human life, so that His children, knowing these laws, could be successful people.

The point (and the goal) here is not about the money at all, but the fact that God's children are called to establish God's Kingdom on this earth, and to show the glory of God here. However, it is simply impossible to do this with limited finances. We need money not only to meet our own needs, but also to fulfill God's plans. God has a preconceived plan for everyone.

Apostle Paul understood this well, and that is why he said:

I am not saying this because I am in need, for I have learned to be content whatever the circumstances. I know what it is to be in

need, and I know what it is to have plenty. I have learned the secret of being content in any and every situation, whether well fed or hungry, whether living in plenty or in want.

Philippians 4:11,12

Paul spoke about money not because he personally was in need of finances. However, he knew that silver answers for everything in this world. He knew that finances are needed for spreading the Kingdom. Many of us, just like Paul, might have lived in want, and in plenty. However, I do not think that anyone of us would say that he prefers poverty.

Some very "spiritual" believers say that the main thing for them is spiritual food. However, while we live in the physical world, we cannot do without physical food, otherwise, our bodies will not be able to function or exist. Denying the necessity of money would be wrong because money is needed to purchase food.

However, we need to know the laws of money so that the need of money does not become a reason for serving it (in stead of God). In addition, we will be able to force money to serve us, as it has been initially planned by God. In this case, we will be able to control money and not depend on it.

Today many people are serving money, although they say they are serving God. This is a paradox. Even those people who have no money still serve money because the only thing they do is thinking of where to earn money to meet the needs of their family. Truly, the person who works for the sake of money is serving money, because he gives a significant part of his time to earning money:

and time is the most vital resource a man has. This opposes God's original plan; it should be quite the opposite. Money should serve us, that is, it should meet our needs and be under our control.

The mentality that it is possible to be live well, be rich and have a lot of money only in developed countries, is mistaken. I would like to say, that money is not a respecter of persons or places. Therefore, it is wrong to say that only Germans or Americans can become rich. No! Money goes to those people who know how it operates. It works for those who know the laws of money. Money goes only to those who can manage it properly.

Every man who desires to glorify God on this earth must have not only a spiritual foundation, which is the most important basis of our life, but also a financial foundation that will enable him to fulfill his dream; the task given to him by God. In order to build this financial foundation, we need to become financially literate; we need to know the laws on how money operates.

THE CULTURE OF SAVINGS

The most important laws of money are the law of reduction of expenses, the law of savings, and the law of economy. Make sure you save between 10% and 30% of any amount of money you receive. Learn to see this saved money as a seed, which you should multiply as much as possible. To do this, you need to invest this money.

Children of God need to prosper financially not because they care only about themselves. They need this to leave an inheritance for the future generations. The Bible confirms this.

A good man leaves an inheritance for his children's children...

Proverbs 13:22

To carry out your calling, you will also need money, as money is the answer for everything *(see: Ecclesiastes 10:19)*. You will not be able to carry out God's plans if you do not have money. This is why every Christian should know and observe the laws of financial prosperity.

It is necessary for every one of us to learn to constantly reduce our expenses. To do so, we need to constantly be able to control our desires. Apostle Paul speaks to his disciple Timothy:

Godliness with contentment is great gain.

1 Timothy 6:6

It is very important to be able to be content with what you have. Some people will never be wealthy and become financially independent, only because they are not content. Their needs always appear bigger than their real incomes. Such people are overcome by greed, gluttony, and hunger. They cannot control their desires, and consequently, their appetite for purchasing different things constantly grows. The person suffering from greediness can never be stably rich. Greediness has ruined the lives of many people who have not been taught to be content with what they had. One car, one house, one wife... were not enough for them. Today many of them have pitiful existence.

If you do not learn to be content with what you have, money will not do you any good. It will become like a hook for you and, most likely, will cause many problems in your life.

The person, who can suppress his appetite for buying, and cut down his expenses, - will be able to direct the saved money to create his financial future. Our needs are endless. Therefore, it is necessary to create a list of the most essential needs, and strictly stick to it, otherwise, our desires will simply ruin us.

Our needs will always try to dictate their conditions to us. They will constantly try to dominate our life. It appears that our needs have their ambitions! Their purpose is to control us. We should keep in mind that the only true Lord of our life is Jesus Christ. We should submit to His laws and rules. Then God will give us many valuable ideas on how to multiply the money we have saved. He will help us in all our financial issues. And then, after some time you will see that a small seed, which you managed to save, has started to bring forth a good harvest.

The truth is that the money we spend on momentary expenses leaves us permanently. However, if we invest our assets, we can receive certain income from them. The money we invest multiplies and brings us even more money.

When we are purchasing something, we are enriching other people. First of all, we should think of how to improve our own financial condition, that is, how to pay ourselves. This is why we should not spend all the money we receive; we should keep a part of it to ourselves! The money we save needs to be sown into a fertile soil as a seed; we need to invest it to benefit us.

Every one of us can start doing something to observe this law of multiplication of money. To start, it is necessary to discipline yourself and limit your needs.

Unfortunately, nobody ever taught most of us this wisdom. We heard nothing about the laws of money from our parents; and even worse; nobody ever told us about them at school. However, having come to God, we should learn His laws and rules of life, which are directed on giving us a life abundantly, which includes abundance in the financial sphere.

Therefore, the culture of savings is the most important condition for financial independence. Many people complain that they have nothing to save or put aside due to big expenses or low salary. However, it is a fact that we always have something to save. Saving will not be a problem, if you approach it seriously and responsibly.

There is an opinion, that the reason for a poor life is lack of money. However, the well-being of a man does not depend on the size of his salary. Everything depends on his skill of managing money. Our well-being is proportional to our savings and expenses. If a person would receive even a million dollars a month, and spend it all, then it is simply impossible for him to become rich. However, even if a man receives only 100 dollars, and regularly saves up a certain percentage of it, then, with time, these small sums will become bigger.

Certainly, discipline in savings begins with faithfulness in giving tithes and offerings. It is necessary to get into the habit of giving "to God what belongs to God" - tithes and offerings, and then it will be easier to discipline yourself in saving.

So, we can find money for savings. First of all, by having a rule: to reduce our expenses daily. Every one of us has expenses, which are absolutely unnecessary. We often spend money on things that are not essential for us. This is the money to be saved.

For example, a person talks too much on the phone daily, buys an extra cup of coffee every day; or instead of using public transportation, he takes a taxi home. Every one of us can make a list of the secondary expenses we spend our money thoughtlessly and carelessly on, daily.

If you reconsider all your daily expenses, I think you will find an opportunity to save five dollars. This seems a very small sum, but if you save 5 dollars a day, then that will be 150 dollars a month worth of savings, and about 2000 dollars a year.

TIME AND CONSISTENCY IN SAVINGS IS THE WAY TO WEALTH

Another law of money says: consistency in savings brings and multiplies wealth. For example, if you constantly put aside some amount of money; if you save it and you do not quit saving; then financial well-being will come into your life eventually.

Many people say that they do not have a big sum of money to put aside as savings. This is a weak argument. As a matter of fact, wealth comes not when we put a large sum of money aside at a time, but when we constantly increase our savings. Thus, wealth comes through consistency in saving small sums.

Time and consistency in savings multiplies money. The point is not in how much money we have, the size of our salary or savings. The point here is in self-discipline and consistency. Will we be able to discipline ourselves to put aside at least 5–10 dollars a day, a week, or a month? If we are going to do this constantly, then we will find out that with time, a small amount of money will turn into great wealth.

Unfortunately, we all know that the more a person earns, the more he usually spends. Therefore, the most suitable time to learn to use your income properly is while it is not so high, as it will be a lot more difficult to do that later.

This is also confirmed in the Bible, where it is written:

As goods increase, so do those who consume them.

Ecclesiastics 5:10

Usually, the temptation to spend money increases with the increase of opportunities of a person. The more money a person has, the stronger the temptation to spend it all. Although, it should be the opposite! It is very important for us to learn to save more as our earnings increase in order to not just keep the money saved by us, but also to multiply it. This will become possible, thanks to time and our consistency.

MULTIPLICATION OF MONEY

If we put the money we saved in a deposit account with 10% annual percentage rate, within 40 years the saved 5 dollars a day will gives us more than a million dollars.

Let's see how you can receive this sum:
In 1 year you will have 1 885 dollars.
In 2 years — 3 967 dollars.
In 5 years — 11 616 dollars.
In 10 years — 30 727 dollars.
In 15 years — 62 171 dollar.
In 30 years — 333 073 dollars.
In 40 years — about 1 million dollars.

Now you see how money is multiplied. This is possible just by putting it in a deposit account in the bank (investing it). If you invest this money in a business (that is, yields not 10% interest per annum, but 30% per annum), then the target of getting one million can be reached not in 40 years, but in 10 years, that is, 4 times faster.

So, in 10–20 years every one of us can really earn a million, thanks to saving 5 dollars a day or 150 dollars a month. The investment plan of depositing a certain sum, which will be constantly multiplied, is clearly shown in the table below.

$300 monthly (saving $10 a day)		$600 monthly (saving $20 a day)		$100 monthly (everyone can do this one)	
DEPOSIT WITH 10% ANNUAL RATE					
1 year	$3,770	1 year	$7,539	1 year	$1,320
2 years	$7,934	2 years	$15,868	2 years	$5,164
5 years	$23,231	5 years	$46,462	5 years	$10,328
10 years	$61,453	10 years	$122,907	10 years	$20,655
15 years	$124,341	15 years	$248,682	15 years	$41,792
30 years	$670,146	30 years	$1,356,293	30 years	$76,570
40 years	$1,897,224	40 years	$3,794,448	40 years	$637, 678

If you keep the saved 100 dollars a month at home, in 40 years, you will only have 48,000 dollars. When you invest it in a bank, thanks to compound interest, time, consistency, and discipline, you will become the owner of a decent sum of money.

Why am I showing you all these figures? This is because figures do not lie. Figures are the facts that speak louder than any words, arguments, excuses and reasoning. You will agree with me, that it is not impossible to become financially free and protected, if you constantly discipline yourself in your financial spending.

Thus, self-discipline is: constantly increase the amount we save regularly, and not touching (spending) it. This is what brings wealth to a man! This is why I said that every Christian can become a rich man, if he really wants to and will start operating according to the financial laws and principles established by God.

You may think or say: "Why do I need money in 40 years, when I may not be alive then?". It is possible, that you will not be alive then, but the principle is this: money is being multiplied with time, and time and consistency are what multiplies it. In any case, your money will remain for your children and grandchildren. Remember, that God advises us to think not only of ourselves.

A good man leaves an inheritance for his children's children...

Proverbs 13:22

If from a young age, a man cares about his financial wellbeing, then he will have a large sum of money when he's old.

If parents start investing in and for their children today, accustoming them to financial discipline, then the financial future of the children will be reliably protected.

Here are golden truths by which every one of us should be guided:

1. Everyone can become a millionaire.
2. Everyone can have a secured future.
3. We always have something to save. Becoming financially independent is the result of a culture of saving.
4. Consistency in savings brings and multiplies wealth.
5. Money is being multiplied with time. Time and consistency in savings is what multiplies it.

Once one brother from our church said a very wise phrase: "What determines our income is not heavy work, but ideas". Only when you change your prototype, your mentality, and attitude toward money, and start applying financial laws into your life, will you definitely become a rich person, in order to reveal Jesus Christ on earth and establish His Kingdom.

FORCE MONEY TO WORK FOR YOU

Force the money you earned to work for you, before you give it away. This is another law of how money works. Unfortunately, the majority of people break this law on a regular basis. Having received a certain amount of money, they immediately give it to other people. In other words, they instantly begin spending the money they just earned. This is the same as giving it away. Those who act like this, enrich others with the money they have earned so hard. Their actions remind me of a railway station: a train, after arriving at a station, has to move on after a short time. As soon as money comes to these people, they pass it on after a short time or right away. They have received it - and they pass it on, received - and pass on, and so on all through their entire life. They actually work as "intermediaries." The majority of people in Ukraine and in other countries live like this.

You need to force money to work for you! Each cent should bring you a dollar before you start spending your earned money. Banks operate on this principle. This is how those who know how to force money to be multiplied act. Money should become "active," and not "passive."

Passive money is the money you earn and spend on different purchases. This money slips through your fingers like water, and unreservedly disappears.

Active money is the money, which brings even more money. That is, it is the money, which is multiplied regardless of you, just because it is invested in something.

To start acting according to the laws of money, we need to change our thinking, because many of us have lived for decades by this principle -received money - gave it away, received it again - gave it away again. It is time for the children of God to change their mentality, which was slavery for a long time, and consequently, made us the slaves of money.

We need to become financially literate in order to destroy a financial yoke. For generations, many peopled worked honestly, but somebody else enjoyed the fruits of their labor. Therefore, the laws on how money works were always hidden from a large population of people.

BUDGET IS THE KEY TO FINANCIAL STABILITY

Financial prosperity is impossible without constant planning and management of money, that is, without a budget. Many people do not even know what a budget is. They are not accustomed to living according to it, and consequently, they always experience a shortage of money. In reality, a budget is intended to help a person to improve his financial situation. We all need to learn to live and work according to a budget.

So how does budgeting help to improve our financial situation? The role of a budget is to help us to separate our needs, desires and necessities. A budget draws a precise dividing line between them, defining the borders of each area of use of money. Usually, only the most vital purchases are put in the budget. In other words, a budget should work on what allows us to live and develop. It helps us to be protected from our own greed or wastefulness.

Often it is possible to hear people making excuses, and having reasons for not having a financial budget. Excuses like, how is it possible to have a budget, if you do not have enough money at all? Such people simply do not want to understand, that the lack of a budget is one of the reasons why they always do not have money. On the other hand, if a person cannot plan small incomes and expenses, how will he be able to manage larger sums of money? It only seems to him, that if money was there, then he would always know how to spend it. However, the truth is that greater money demands greater skill to manage it. Therefore, God cannot bless many of us, because we cannot manage money properly.

Making a budget is an art. Therefore, every one of us needs to study it in order not to only become financially protected, but also teach our children, grandchildren, and other children of God about it.

Many Christians just pray for God to bless them with finances. But there is no money in heaven. God cannot hand the requested amount of money directly over into our hands, because He is in heaven, and we are on earth. However, He can give His children wisdom on how to earn and multiply money. He can reveal the secrets of multiplying money to us, but He will do nothing for us. If we remain inactive or break His laws, then we ourselves will be guilty of the fact that God's promises, for some reasons, do not work in our life.

Some people often accuse our church "The embassy of God" of teaching our people how to become rich. We do so, and we will continue to teach people financial literacy, so that they can glorify God on earth not only with their words, but also with their finances. These finances are received, thanks to God's wisdom and the knowledge of His laws, by which money not only exists, but is also multiplied.

Money is not just a means for payments. First of all, money is a seed, which should bring a plentiful harvest. However, the question is: do we use money as a seed? Do we know the laws of the growth of a monetary seed? Do we know how to find a fertile soil for sowing?

God does not want us to be in need, but we should know the laws of financial prosperity, so that we can then thank God for His plentiful financial blessings.

MAIN CONDITION FOR KEEPING WEALTH

Today, many people in the world manage to save significant amounts of money in their bank accounts. However, not all of those people, who have a lot of money, can be called rich. It often happens that money easily received is also easily lost by its owner. Only the one, who knows the principles of real wealth and observes them, can be confident of his financial condition. If a person lives and operates according to the laws of God, he will always have a guarantee against unforeseen situations. His life is always predictable, and therefore he faces any unexpected turns of destiny fully prepared.

The researches of the lives of many stably successful people, who possess real wealth show that all of them were people, who have devoted a significant part of their life time to self-improvement. They were the people, who have been working hard developing themselves, people with strict discipline, who did not allow themselves to break moral principles.

These people were able to keep huge amounts of money in their possession, because they have overcome greed, lust of the flesh, lust of the eyes, and pride of life. They are people, who have a large amount of money in their possession but did not rush to buy everything available in the best shops or own the best houses, cars, women, etc.

They strictly observed the balance between their incomes and expenses, repeatedly multiplying their money, instead of spending it to satisfy their own lusts.

That is why they could keep it for a long time, and pass it on to future generations in their family.

Truly wealthy people differ from others by the fact that they could overcome pride. Their wealth does not give them a reason to be exalted over other people.

So, the people who own stable riches were able to overcome themselves, and this is the main condition for keeping wealth. Only the person, who can overcome himself can become a real wealthy person. You should lose taste for money, things, and success to become really wealthy. You should have absolute control over yourself. Otherwise, before you will manage to become rich, riches will destroy you. If you are not able to be self-controlled, riches will constantly escape from your hands.

The Word of God teaches us that we should take control over all our actions and even thoughts. We should act according to the spirit, not by flesh - as worldly people do by habit. Therefore, the Bible says:

Like a city whose walls are broken down is a man who lacks self-control.

Proverbs 25:28

This is the strongest comparison. During the reign of king Solomon, the author of the Book of Proverbs, there were strong walls around the cities, which protected inhabitants from numerous enemies. The city without walls represented a completely defenseless city, which could be robbed by anybody.

A man who is not self-controlled, who is not able to take control of his spirit, is similar to such a defenseless city. He can easily be robbed in the middle of the day. This will not be done by robbers, but by his own inability to be self-controlled, his inability to control his desires and feelings.

As soon as a person gets a lot of money, his sight becomes "sharper" - he starts noticing what he has not seen before. If you have a million dollars, you suddenly begin to notice how fine and elegant the suits that cost several thousands of dollars are. You are already such a rich person that wearing something cheaper is not prestigious to you anymore! You do not want to drive your old car anymore, because you see that other people have finer new cars. The list of your purchases which seem a priority to you can be endless, but the truth is that only the person who can control himself, who can control his constantly growing desires, can have real wealth.

People say that the person who indulges his desires has a hole in his wallet. As you understand, the point is not in how old the wallet is, but in the wallet constantly being drained by the irrepressible desires of the owner; therefore, money does not stay there. His money simply gets lost, same as thrown out to the wind, as it happens to the person, whose wallet really has a hole in it.

Unfortunately today, the majority of people work for a "holey" wallet. Everything earned by them is immediately spent on different essential and unnecessary things, which these people could have lived without. Such people will never become rich, even if they get a large amount of money. They will rather quickly spend it on restaurants, clothes, and other entertainments.

Therefore, the major principle of obtaining real wealth can be possessed only by a person who can control himself. Certainly, this is not easy, and requires certain efforts from a man. As mentioned earlier in the Book of Proverbs, the person, who cannot control his spirit, is comparable to a vulnerable, defenseless city without walls, which is in constant danger. Just like building city walls requires hard work, so does cultivating self-control in money management is also a hard work.

A man who plans to have real and long-lasting wealth will also need to put a lot of effort to change his character. Character is a tool for protecting what you have earned. It is a well-known fact that it is a lot easier to earn money than to keep it. If a person does not have strong character and cannot control himself, it means that he will not be able to protect his wealth from his endless desires. The person who develops himself, improving his character, can become not just a millionaire, but a stably rich person as well. He will not only be able to get riches, but he will keep them and multiply them, constantly controlling his desires and lusts.

To develop a strong character and learn self-control is a task that any of us can do because every man has the best personal qualities in him. We just need to discover and develop them. We need to develop new skills and abilities, using the reserves hidden in us. Then, we will be able to learn not to be reactive to money (which the Lord is going to bless us with), and stop seeing it as a tool for satisfying our desires and lusts.

So, self-development is a major principle of having real wealth. Certainly, you may ask: what connection is there between self-development and wealth? The connection between them is very direct. If a person has overcome the desire of wastefulness, this speaks about his self-discipline, self-development. In this case, he has the ability to keep the money.

Money rules this world, that is, mammon - the spirit of riches. Many people long for riches to satisfy the lusts of their flesh. Believers long for riches too, but they have absolutely different goals. They need riches, in order not to be "cooler" than others, not to have everything their souls want. They need riches to establish God's Kingdom on earth.

To do this, they would need to start by setting themselves free from worldly motivations, and approach this question with God's wisdom. They should learn to manage money, and not allow it to manage them. They should be set free from any control of money. For this purpose, it is necessary to know the laws and principles, by which money exists and is multiplied.

The life of the people who love God is submitted to God in the same way the life of those who love money is submitted to money. Money has a way of managing people, and many of them are in slavery to mammon. Only a man, who can manage himself, can overcome this idol called money. Those who worship it think that they own money, but actually, money owns them.

It is very easy to check, whether money has an authority over you or not. What do you do, if money comes to you? If you immediately run to the store or market to spend it quickly, then that is proof that money owns you and not vice versa. Consequently, you will never become rich, as you are not taught to control yourself and the money you receive.

YOUR WEALTH IS DETER-MINED BY THE QUALITY OF YOUR SERVICE TO PEOPLE

One more principle of finding real wealth is the ability to serve other people. This is what true business is all about. Every person who wants to be engaged in business needs to truly realize this.

Many people do not understand the purpose of business. Some of them think that business is an opportunity to find financial prosperity, to earn and save a large amount of money. Some people, out of ignorance, call robbing, cheating, swindling, or plundering a business. However, real business is certain services rendered by a person.

Certainly, a rightly established business can bring enduring wealth to a person. However, this is only a consequence, that is, a result, but not the purpose of a business. Its purpose, as mentioned, is to serve people. Business is an opportunity to use your abilities and talents, to release your potential, in order to give an answer and satisfy the needs of people.

Unfortunately, we should admit that many modern businessmen are simply speculators, as the quality of their services does not correspond with the price they demand for these services. Such businessmen have a wrong view of business, and consequently, their wealth will never be durable and enduring.

It does not matter what industry your business is in, it could be trade, aircraft construction, or medical. Any business is a service. Business is, first of all, the desire of a person to serve others. Wealth received as a result of operating the business is only a reward for excellent and diligent services. This is how God sees business.

You can achieve the stability of wealth through proper management of your business. High quality of the services offered provides an uninterrupted stream of consumers of these services. And naturally, the more buyers or clients a businessman has, the richer he becomes.

The size of your wealth and its stability is defined by the quantity of the people you serve. In other words, your wealth is defined by the quantity of the people you were able to provide excellent and diligent service to.

Manufacturers of poor-quality goods or services will eventually lose their consumers, and eventually their riches as well. It is possible to deceive a small amount of people for a small period of time. However, it is impossible to deceive all people all the time. Deception cannot last forever.

Quality always attracts people and increases demand. As demand increases, even more will be the number of people wishing to take advantage of an excellent service or product. The more people you serve, the richer you become and your wealth will become more stable as well.

The more people you serve, the higher you can rise. This is why the Bible says:

Whoever wants to become great among you must be your servant, and whoever wants to be first must be slave of all.

Mark 10:43,44

Your wealth depends on your ability to present an excellent and diligent service to as many people as possible. Excellent and diligent service is what true business is all about - this is the way God sees business.

A business rendering an excellent service is an expression of God's love. True business is built on the law of love, which says, treat others as you want them to treat you. This is the main foundation for quality for any business.

Just selling the product does not necessarily mean that you are providing a (good) service. If you do not put your attitude of love into the person this product is intended for, then you are not a businessman, but just a dealer. Your understanding of what business is, will change your attitude to your consumer, and will also change the condition of your business. Diligent and excellent service will inevitably lead you to wealth and glory. If you look at your business, not as an opportunity for accumulating wealth, but as an opportunity for diligent service to people, you will not need to search for riches - they will come to you by themselves.

So, wealth is a compensation for the diligent and excellent service given in love to a man. Everyone to a certain degree is a businessman because God has put the ability and desire to serve people in love into everybody. God has given the ability to love and be loved to every person. A loving person always possesses the qualities of a giver. So, if you can give something to other people, that means, you are serving them. Service is the essence of business, and if you are serving someone, that means, you are a businessman.

Every person has something he can serve people with. This service can become a foundation of his business. There are numerous ideas in us, which have great prospects. Children of God cannot be broke. Only laziness and unwillingness to work can prevent them from becoming successful and rich people. Everything that is necessary for achieving stable success and wealth is already incorporated into us by God. We just need to start taking action by serving people in love, and by doing this, we are glorifying God on earth.

Many Christians think that God gives His children wealth but, that is a distorted view. The Bible says that God gives the power (strength) to get (gain) riches. He does not give wealth, He gives the ability to acquire wealth. You need to get riches, and to do this, you need to put certain efforts (ability) into it. So, that is the problem of believers, who, after coming to God, stop working, only hoping for God's blessings.

God will give us the power (strength) to get riches. Nevertheless, there is a great gap between power to get riches and getting riches. The power to get riches is not equal to riches. In other words, the fact that you have an ability to be wealthy does not mean that you will automatically become rich. Your ability is only a deposit, that if you put efforts, you can obtain riches through it. To have wealth, you need to obtain it. This is a whole process that requires a desire to serve people in love with the abilities and talents, which the Lord has generously given to you.

So, the principles of financial prosperity we spoke about in this chapter are the following:

- The principle of giving;
- The principle of savings;
- The principle of planning and managing;
- The principle of multiplication;

- The principle of self-improvement;
- The principle of service to people.

SECURE YOUR FUTURE

Anybody, who knows and applies the laws of financial prosperity, can become rich and wealthy. Certainly, it would be naive to hope that knowing the laws alone will make you rich. Not at all! We need to put certain efforts into it. However, it is not too difficult to become rich - you just need to become a doer, and not be a person who only has financial knowledge.

At the time of writing, Ukraine is aspiring to enter the European union, and we, believers, should be prepared to accept the fact that during the periods of global changes some people in the society will become victims. However, these victims should not be Christians, not me and you! This is why we need to know how to provide for ourselves, for our retirement, and the life of our children.

The Bible says, that **"...money is the answer for everything"** *(Ecclesiastics 10:19)*. Therefore, it would be unwise to deny that we need money for attaining the goals the Lord has set before us.

Many Christians think that they should not have anything in common with riches or wealth, but the Bible says, that **"a good man leaves an inheritance for his children's children..."** *(Proverbs 13:22)*. Undoubtedly, it is impossible for a lazy and disobedient man to become rich. Only the person, who really wants to find financial safety during this uncertain time, will surely attain the goal, if he thoroughly studies the laws of money to provide for his future and the future of his descendants.

GOLDEN TRUTHS

- Giving tithes alone is not enough for financial prosperity.
- Money functions under its laws.
- Money does not go only to those who go to church, it goes to those who know and comply with the laws of money.
- We need money not only for meeting our own needs, but also for fulfilling God's plans.
- The person, who works for the sake of gaining money, is serving money.
- Our needs will always try to dictate their conditions to us.
- When we purchase something, we are enriching other people.
- Money needs to be sown into a fertile soil as a seed. We need to invest it for it to benefit us.
- Our well-being is proportional to our savings and expenses.
- Time and consistency in savings multiplies money.
- The temptation to spend money increases as a person's opportunities increase.
- Every Christian can become a rich person.
- Your money should become active, not passive.
- Financial prosperity is impossible without constant planning and management of money.

- Money is a seed, which should bring a plentiful harvest.
- The power to get riches is not equal to getting riches.
- Only the person, who can overcome himself, can become really wealthy.
- The more people you serve, the higher you can rise.
- Every person has something he can serve other people with.

10

THE LAWS OF THE BODY

THE "LOAN" GIVEN TO US BY GOD

Life is given to everyone as a demonstration of God's trust. It does not belong to us. It is a kind of loan, given to us by God. The life, we have received is like a lease. It represents the unity of the spirit, soul and body, which require constant care.

If God has given each one of us a body, would He want us to neglect it? God knows how important the body is for our existence on earth; therefore, He wants us to take adequate care of it.

Don't you know that you yourselves are God's temple and that God's Spirit lives in you?

1 Corinthians 3:16

Do you not know that your body is a temple of the Holy Spirit, who is in you, whom you have received from God? You are not your own;

1 Corinthians 6:19

Taking care of the body is very important for every Christian because the Holy Spirit lives in our bodies. The body of a Christian is actually a house where God lives.

Imagine what would happen if the President of Ukraine, America, or any other country, is coming to your city. The city authorities would immediately start to meticulously prepare for this event. There will be thorough cleaning of the streets, painting of the facades of houses, and so on. What if that influential person would be staying in the city for a long time? I think you can imagine how thoroughly the city authorities would work hard to see that the sanitary condition and the buildings in the city are in good condition, and that law enforcement is on a high level.

If a president is met with such honor and preparation, then how should you prepare for the almighty God Who desires to live in your body? He desires to make your body His temple, a place of His dwelling. How much more thoroughly should you take care of your body, where God lives? You cannot afford to treat it carelessly. Certainly, every one of us should take good care of his body - the flesh, through which God wants to operate on this earth

THE BODY IS THE DWELLING OF THE SPIRIT

Every man should know and observe the physiological laws of our flesh to live a meaningful life on earth. This book does not set a goal of making a scientific research of these laws. However, we will look at the Biblical point of view on the laws of flesh, the law of human body.

As stated in the Bible, man was created in God's image and likeness.

> **Then God said, "Let us make man in our image, in our likeness, and let them rule over the fish of the sea and the birds of the air, over the livestock, over all the earth, and over all the creatures that move along the ground."**
>
> *Genesis 1:26*

God is a Trinity; He is the father, Son and Holy Spirit. Man is a trinity as well: he has a spirit, soul and body. God is a Spirit. A true man also is a spirit that lives in a physical body (the flesh). Man is created by God to live on earth, in a material dimension. For this reason, he cannot live and operate on this planet outside of a body.

Everything that exists on earth is subject to certain laws. The body of a man cannot exist outside these laws; it is also subject to them. Observing certain laws, a man will keep his body in proper condition.

The body is intended for a man to be able to have contact with the physical world and carry out certain actions. The real man is a spirit, but the material body

165

has been given to him to operate on earth in order to use the potential which has been initially incorporated into him by God. In other words, we can say that the body is a dwelling of the spirit. Actually, the body is a material environment of the spirit, which a true man is.

TAKING CARE OF THE BODY IS A NECESSARY CONDITION FOR FULFILLING GOD'S CALLING

However, this does not mean that the flesh can be neglected and treated carelessly. A body is like a house where the spirit lives. It is known that any house requires care. Some people calling themselves believers totally neglect their bodies. Their nutrition is inappropriate, they do not pay attention to how they dress, they do not care for their health, and this upset God.

No matter how spiritual a man could be, if his body is becoming weak and cannot function normally, he will be useless for God. Such person will not be able to use his potential and fulfill the plan of God for his earthly life.

This is why, every one of us needs to take care not only of our spiritual development and growth, but our bodies as well. This is why we need to do sport, have enough rest and on time, and have a balanced diet. We need to live for a long time in the body given to us to fulfill God's plan on earth.

The body is given to us by God to fulfill His plan, and therefore, we should treat it responsibly. We should learn to constantly take care of it because fulfilling what we have been called to do, depends it. a strong spirit cannot live in a weak body. A sick and ailing flesh is not capable of demonstrating God's greatness on earth. The weakness of the human body sometimes hinders God from fulfilling His business on earth. That is why we cannot be indifferent to the condition of our flesh. We should ensure that our bodies are healthy and strong; worthy for God, Who created us to live therein. Therefore, an excuse for not taking care of our bodies cannot be the lack of money and time.

TWO EXTREMES

The word "flesh" has two meanings. On one hand, it means our physical body, and on the other, the fallen nature of man.

People tend to have two extremes relating to their bodies. One of them is that, they do not consider it necessary to take care of their body at all. Many Christians are in this category; they think that, after coming to God, they should only take care of their spirit. Therefore, they do not pay any attention to the condition their bodies. Having this wrong view, they think that they are showing their modesty in this way. Actually, by not caring about how they look, these people are simply dishonoring and extremely upsetting God.

Christians should always look decent because they are the representatives of God on earth. They are already cleansed within; therefore, they should look accordingly on the outside. Some people dress nicely, only when they are visiting their friends, but they do not care how they look when they go to God, that is, to the church.

Of course, there is also another extreme, when some people do not care about their inside condition, spending all of their time to take care for their outward appearance. They please their body and only take care of it. Such people long to earn as much money as possible to spend on the needs of their bodies. This is the reason for which they live. The meaning of life for them is in this. Their life goes on in search of fine and exotic food, the most fashionable and expensive clothes, shoes, perfumes and other attributes of luxury.

The devil confuses people, drawing their attention to what is insignificant in life, and distracting them from God.

Everything should be balanced in our life and in our desire to look decent, we should watch out for our hearts not to be attached to it. Our attention should be concentrated on God, instead of concentrating on what we wear. Therefore, the Bible says:

...Man does not live on bread alone, but on every word that comes from the mouth of God.

Matthew 4:4

FLESH SHOULD BE SUBMITTED TO THE SPIRIT

The life of a man, who does not know God, is guided by the desires of his flesh. He satisfies all its lusts.

The acts of the sinful nature are obvious: sexual immorality, impurity and debauchery; Idolatry and witchcraft; hatred, discord, jealousy, fits of rage, selfish ambition, dissensions, factions And envy; drunken-

ness, orgies, and the like. I warn you, as I did before, that those who live like this will not inherit the kingdom of God.

Galatians 5:19-21

If a person's life is guided by the needs of his body, he will be gradually separated from God. This happened in the garden of Eden, when eve, having given in to the desire of flesh, disobeyed God, and sinned. Sin always leads to death - the Bible speaks about it:

For the wages of sin is death...

Romans 6:23

The believer, who wants to know God, longs to live by the spirit and by the fruits of the spirit, which the Bible speaks about:

But the fruit of the Spirit is love, joy, peace, patience, kindness, goodness, faithfulness, gentleness and self-control.

Galatians 5:22,23

A man who has a strong spirit obtains the strength to go against the lusts of the flesh. The flesh does not dictate its conditions to such a person anymore, because it is submitted to the spirit. The person is driven by the spirit in his life, he is guided by the instructions of the Holy Spirit and consequently, he is capable of fulfilling God's will.

For the spirit to be strong, we should strengthen it by God's Word, prayer and fasting. Without this, we will not be able to take care of the body properly. Only by having a strong spirit, can we control the desires of the flesh. We should also be careful not to turn taking care of the flesh into giving in to its lusts, which can destroy our soul.

So I say, live by the Spirit, and you will not gratify the desires of the sinful nature...

Galatians 5:16

The world around us lives by the desires of the flesh. This world is ruled by the lust of the flesh, lust of eyes, and pride of life. God's children should live by the spirit, and not give a place to the devil in their lives. The devil will definitely try to attack us through the desires of the flesh.

That is why apostle Paul spoke:

Those who belong to Christ Jesus have cruci-fied the sinful nature with its passions and desires.

Galatians 5:24

Paul spoke not only about the whole body of Christ, but also about himself personally:

...No, I beat my body and make it my slave so that after I have preached to others, I myself will not be disqualified for the prize.

1 Corinthians 9:27

The great apostle said that every day, he tried to over-come his flesh by the spirit. Paul knew that by overcoming his fleshly thoughts, he overcame the devil, whose purpose is to destroy our relationships with God.

It is said in the Bible, that we are already crucified with Christ.

> **...For we know that our old self was crucified with him so that the body of sin might be done away with, that we should no longer be slaves to sin – Because anyone who has died has been freed from sin.**
>
> *Romans 6:6,7*

A true Christian will not allow himself to live by the dictation of the flesh. The flesh should be ruled by the born again spirit, which desires to show obedience to the Lord.

PROPER DIET IS A GUARANTEE FOR LONG LIFE

Long life for a man is impossible without keeping the laws of the flesh. The law of proper and balanced diet also belongs to these laws of the flesh. In spite of the fact that in the new Testament, there are no special restrictions on specific foods, nevertheless, God expects us to be wise in choosing the food we eat. Therefore He says to us:

> **Everything is permissible for me-but not everything is beneficial. Everything is permissible for me - but I will not be mastered by anything.**
>
> *1 Corinthians 6:12*

171

Even if you pray a lot and try to observe all of God's commandments, it does not guarantee you long life if you know nothing about the laws of the flesh and do not observe them. The laws of nutrition, the laws of rest, and laws of movement belong to these laws. Whoever does not observe these laws is killing himself, even if he is a very spiritual person or an anointed minister.

For example, I did not pay attention to my diet at all some years ago. When I got married, I noticed that my wife's diet was different from mine. She observed certain rules, that is, laws. I did not know these laws, and therefore my food consumption was always chaotic. However, when I started reading books on nutrition, I found out that I was causing damage to my own health by not knowing the laws of nutrition. Being ignorant of these laws was destroying my life.

Taking good care of the flesh is an important duty of every believer, who wants to fulfill God's plan. Therefore, every one of us should analyze our attitude toward our flesh, which has been given to us as a dwelling for the spirit. We should make sure that we are doing everything possible for it to be able to serve God and establish His Kingdom on earth for many years.

GOLDEN TRUTHS

- Life is given to everyone as a demonstration of God's trust.
- The body is intended for a man to be able to have contact with the physical world and fulfill certain actions.
- The body is a dwelling of the spirit.
- The body is given to us by God for the fulfillment of His plan.
- Our attention should be concentrated on God, instead of on what we wear.
- A man who does not know God lives guided by the desires of his flesh.
- Having a strong spirit, we can control the desires of the flesh.
- Long life for a man is impossible without keeping the laws of the flesh.

11

ANY LAW WORKS FOR OUR GOOD

All the laws of life, by which life on earth is created, are established to protect man from all possible problems and difficulties. These laws work for our good; therefore, we should know and observe them. In this chapter, we will take a look at some more very important laws people encounter every day. Understanding these laws makes our life comfortable and eliminates any anxiety, fear and disappointment.

THE LAW OF ATTRACTION

The law of attraction, which is also called the law of magnetism, states that whatever you are meditating on is drawn to you. What you think about defines your life.

... For as he thinks within himself, so he is...

Proverbs 23:7

The law of attraction says that a man becomes his thoughts. The things a man appreciates and values are always drawn to him.

For example, if you admire a preacher, you will definitely try not to miss his sermons. You will be interested in listening to him, and start receiving what he has to offer. His internal riches which have attracted you to him will become your treasure, because you will meditate upon what you hear from him. What you have appreciated in this person will become yours.

However, if you disregard this person and fail to appreciate him, you will never have what he possesses.

What you value becomes yours, so says the law of attraction. If you neglect finances, you will always be poor. On the other hand, if you understand its value, and keep the laws of finance, your income will significantly increase because by meditating upon the value of money, you will find a way to change your financial condition.

Do not expect something you do not appreciate to come to your life. If you want to have something, you must start appreciating and honoring it. Live by what is important to you, and it will really become yours. You draw to yourself, what you honor. This is the result of the law of attraction.

This law also states that similar things are drawn to each other. It means that the person, who constantly argues or criticizes other people, will be around the same kind of people as himself. The person who is always easily filled with envy gets along with other envious people.

The person who stands by the truth will be surrounded by those who do not lie, because birds of the same feather flock together.

Your inner condition draws the same kind of people to you. Your inner essence, your internal values will definitely draw people with similar values to you. If you are a holy and righteous person, you will definitely be fellowshipping with similar people. They will be invisibly drawn to you as a result of the law of attraction.

The law of attraction states that the actions of man's thoughts are similar to the action of a magnet. They have the ability to draw the things the man thinks about. Therefore, if we want to be surrounded by good people, then we should be good people ourselves. The person who is filled with love and goodness will draw love and goodness to himself. The person who thinks of peace and appreciates peace in relationships with people will never be surrounded by those who like arguing and scandals.

THE LAW OF THE FLIP SIDE OF A COIN

Some people call this law "the law of parallel" or "the law of objectivity." What is the essence of this law? It states that everything visible has a flip side, like a coin. We should not judge everything in the same way, stating that it is good or bad. There is a flip side of the coin in every life's situation. What is good for one person can appear bad for someone else.

Therefore, when there are conflicts between people, we should not listen to the opinion of only one party. We should not make a conclusion based on the opinion of only one person; instead, we should listen to other opinions about the case. They can be absolutely opposite. It is always necessary to keep in mind that there is a flip side of the coin to any case, thing or situation.

It does not matter how bad your situation may seem to you. The main thing for you is to look at it from another perspective. In fact, according to the law of the flip side of a coin, it is possible to see some good things in any bad situation.

If you were abandoned by your husband, remember that there is another side of the coin, which is not yet visible to you. If you have lost your job, do not be upset, because every situation has a flip side of the coin. Most likely, a much more interesting and lucrative opportunity is waiting for you. So there are no reasons for tears and sorrow, if you know the law of the flip side of a coin. Even death, which is often perceived by the majority of people as a tragedy of life, has a flip side. Nobody ever knows if it would really be better for the deceased to remain alive.

Knowing the law of the flip side of a coin, you will always be able to see something positive where other people see only bad things. For this reason, we cannot judge other people in a negative way, because every one of us has a flip side of the coin as well. Therefore, do not be hasty to make conclusions about someone, but try to learn more about him to see not only his bad sides, but good sides as well. Every person has both good and bad sides. Everything in this life has a flip side of the coin.

According to this law, we should never rush with decision-making. Any situation or offer should be considered from different angles. Good and obviously beneficial offers should be critically analyzed. Any contract beneficial for you will also always have a flip side to it. If you do not investigate it thoroughly, then you may give it a wrong estimation and as a result, make a mistake.

Sometimes, the law of the flip side of a coin is also called the law of objectivity. This law was used by the wise king of Israel, Solomon when he had to solve a controversial issue, when he was approached by two women. Each one insisted that the living child belonged to her. After listening to both women and thoroughly investigating the issue, Solomon asked the women a wise question, which solved this unusual dispute.

Now two prostitutes came to the king and stood before him. One of them said, "My lord, this woman and I live in the same house. I had a baby while she was there with me. The third day after my child was born; this woman also had a baby. We were alone; there was no one in the house but the two of us. During the night this woman's son died because she lay on him. So she got up in the middle of the night and took my son from my side while I your servant was asleep. She put him by her breast and put her dead son by my breast. The next morning, I got up to nurse my son—and he was dead! But when I looked at him closely in the morning light, I saw that it wasn't the son I had borne." The other woman said, "No! The living one is my son; the dead one is yours." But the first one insisted, "No! The dead one is yours; the living one is mine." And so they argued

before the king. The king said, "This one says, "My son is alive and your son is dead," while that one says, "No! Your son is dead and mine is alive." Then the king said, "Bring me a sword." So they brought a sword for the king. He then gave an order: "Cut the living child in two and give half to one and half to the other." The woman whose son was alive was filled with compassion for her son and said to the king, "Please, my lord, give her the living baby! Don't kill him!" But the other said, "Neither I nor you shall have him. Cut him in two!" Then the king gave his ruling: "Give the living baby to the first woman. Do not kill him; she is his mother." When all Israel heard the verdict the king had given, they held the king in awe, because they saw that he had wisdom from God to administer justice.

1 Kings 3:16-28

A wise man is always constrained in decision-making because he remembers God's laws. That is why King Solomon, known all over the world for his wisdom, said:

He who answers before listening – that is his folly and his shame.

Proverbs 18:13

The law of the flip side of a coin is not just about the fact that every coin has two sides. This law states that these two sides are opposite and absolutely equal. They have equal rights to exist. it talks about the right of pluralism, that is, the existence of opposite opinions. Life is full of contrasts.

> **And the LORD God made all kinds of trees grow out of the ground—trees that were pleasing to the eye and good for food. In the middle of the garden were the tree of life and the tree of the knowledge of good and evil.**
>
> *Genesis 2:9*

As we see, good and evil are real, that is, contrast exists; so we should be able to distinguish what is good and what is evil. We should not be naive and allow people to deceive us.

Very often it happens that we are let down by people who call themselves "believers," and probably even go to your church. It is always necessary to remember that going to church is just one side of a person's life. In addition, it does not mean at all, that it is the only side of his life. Each person has another side of life, which can be absolutely unknown to us. Therefore, thorough analysis is always needed before drawing any conclusion about a particular person.

The law of the flip side of a coin states that facts are always required to draw conclusions and make serious decisions. It is possible to judge a situation or a person only when our judgments are based on concrete facts. Allow facts to draw conclusions for you. In any disputable situation, the facts given from both parties will allow you to come to consensus.

THE CREATIVE FORCE
OF DISCONTENT

It happens quite often that we are dissatisfied with something in our life. This means that God wants to do something greater through us. When we feel dissatisfied with our life, and for some reason nothing satisfies nor gives us joy anymore, this means that God, who lives inside of us, wants to tell us that we are capable of something greater and we can do much more than what we are doing now. We have enough opportunities, abilities and potential to do so. When discontent is born inside of us, that means that God, who is living in us, desires to manifest Himself more through us. By suppressing God's life within us, we disobey Him and this leads to depression.

Discontent has a creative force in it. This is a result of the law of the other side of the coin. If a man knows the reason for his discontent, he will try to give God the opportunity to manifest through him in a new way. He will be obedient to God's will, and consequently, start doing something new in his life - something that God wants to be done. The person who does not know the reason for his internal dissatisfaction will go into deeper depression. In order to suppress the feeling of dissatisfaction, some people start using alcohol or drugs on regular basis, and as a result they fall into dependency on them. These people, in search of a solution to their problem, find a false way out, and the situation will not change until they become obedient to God and live by His laws.

If you allow God to work through you to the full extent, through your abilities, talents, thoughts and ideas, you will not have any limitation. The scale of your growth would be limitless. The principle of a seed (that is, the repeated multiplication of a seed that is sown) would start to operate in this case. Just as a seed that has grown brings forth fruits, so will a man who accepts God's ideas and thoughts, and is obedient to God's will, will start receiving and using more ideas. One completed work of God generates more works. Fruitfulness is always hidden in a seed. It is the law of God; His principle.

Often, when feeling discontent, we begin to search for its reason in our relatives, co-workers, friends, and church members. We have the tendency to find explanations for our problems in some physical objects, but actually, there can be only one explanation for our discontent - we have "constrained" the life of God within us. This does not satisfy God at all; He longs to be revealed through us actively, that is, He wants to operate through us.

God is the Creator, He is constantly creating. The Lord said to His disciples:

Jesus said to them, "My Father is always at his work to this very day, and I, too, am working."

John 5:17

Jesus Christ understands the movement of God. He perfectly realizes that He should not ignore this movement. If the father is in Him, and He is constantly creating, that means, the Son, too, should continue to constantly create.

When you allow God to manifest through you, you will experience a great joy because by doing so, you will eliminate any contradiction between the life of God inside you and your personal life.

Jesus Christ was never in a bad mood, as He operated in agreement with God. In other words, He was always doing what God wanted to do.

If God is in us, and we are in Him, then we should constantly receive something from Him, express what we have received from Him, and create what He desires to create. The life of God in us gives us energy for creation. If we do not use this energy, it will cause us to have a feeling of discontent.

The potential and opportunities of the person, who is obedient to God in this process of creation, will constantly grow because the person who is faithful in little will definitely receive greater blessing.

The person who does not meet God's expectations has no right to look forward to God's blessings. Today, God will not open a new door for someone who has not used or taken advantage of a door that was opened yesterday. We should be obedient to His desires - for them to operate and be manifested through us; only then will we have no limitations in carrying out what was planned by God.

So, our discontent with ourselves and life around us has a flip side of the coin. It testifies that the time of changes should come into our life. If we know the laws of life well, then along with God's wisdom and advice, we will start searching for new opportunities which God has already prepared for our advancement.

THE LAW OF RELATIVITY

The law of relativity states that everything is relative in this life. This means that not everything is as bad as it may seem to us. The condition you are in right now is not as bad as you think. You just have to compare yourself with someone else, whose circumstances are a lot worse than yours.

The law of relativity teaches us that everything is comprehended in comparison. Probably, your financial situation might not be worth writing home about. But if you compare yourself to somebody who is rich, but very sick, you will realize that you have many things to be thankful to God for. Perhaps, today you are sick, but you can hear, see and speak. Remember how many people in the world are deprived of such opportunities, and you will understand that you have a reason for joy and gratitude to God. Always thank Him for the air you breathe and your nose with which you breathe. Be thankful for the mouth you have to eat. Be thankful for the ears you can hear with. Be thankful for your hands you can work with, for your legs, which you use to walk on this earth. Regardless of how complex the situation you are in may seem to you, remember that everything is comprehended and viewed in comparison. In addition, it means that everything is rather good in your life. God is good and merciful, and therefore you can always enjoy life if you apply the law of relativity.

The truth is comprehended only in comparison. In other words, your true situation will be found out only when you compare it to other people's situations. There are some people today, who are doing worse than you. Thus, you can help them somehow.

The law of relativity teaches us to not concentrate on our problems because they are relative. Therefore, search for somebody who needs your help and after doing that, you will forget about your temporary problems which seemed so complex to you.

The law of relativity states that there is nothing too fast or too slow, there is nothing small or big; because in comparison with something else the big can appear small, and what is completely small can appear greater. Fast can become slow, when you compare it to something faster. In addition, what was slow can appear pretty fast, if you compare it to something that is not moving at all.

This law states that life is always relative, depending on what you compare it to. It also teaches us that we will always meet two kinds of people in this life: those who are better than us, so that we could imitate them and learn from them; and those who are worse than us, so that we could help them, and be a kind and positive example for them. When we see someone who is in a worse condition than us, we can minister to that person and help him to solve his problem. If we see that there is someone better than us, it is a good opportunity for us to humble ourselves and realize that we are still not as good as we thought we were.

The law of relativity, as well as other laws, works for our good, as it helps us to long for the best, because perfection has no limit. It gives us a reason for joy, because even a complex situation appears insignificant in comparison, therefore there are no reasons for sorrow. We can always find a reason to thank God and be happy. We should live a life of worship and gratitude to God.

Knowing the laws the life on earth is based on, we will always be happy with this life that has been generously given to us by God.

GOLDEN TRUTHS

- All laws work for our good; therefore, we should know and observe them.
- What you think about defines your life.
- What you value becomes yours.
- Similar things are drawn to each other.
- The actions of man's thoughts are similar to the action of a magnet.
- Everything visible has a flip side, like a coin.
- Any situation or offer should be considered from different angles.
- A wise man is always constrained in decision-making.
- Life is full of contrasts.
- Facts are always required to draw conclusions and make serious decisions.
- Discontent has a creative force in it.
- Your true situation will be found out only when you compare it to other people's situations.
- The person who does not meet God's expectations has no right to expect God's blessings.
- Everything is comprehended in comparison.
- When you allow God to be manifested through you, you will experience a great joy.

12

CREATE YOUR FUTURE

YOU ARE THE OWNER OF YOUR LIFE

There are two ways of life that lead to the peak of a meaningful life. One of them is through hard work. The second way is easier, it is based on knowing the laws of life and using other people's experience. Though, this also requires work but it is easier to attain success using this method than using the first one. Knowing the laws of life makes life predictable and learning from the experience of other people helps to avoid making many mistakes.

The future of every one of us is in our own hands. It does not depend on politicians, economic condition, or the result of another election. It depends only on us. It depends on our purposes and how we want to attain them. It depends on how much we are ready for this life and what we want to see in it. It depends on how well we know and observe the laws of life.

Life is a battle. Therefore, every one of us should fight for our future and success. We should be able to build our life ourselves and to do this, we need to know the laws that life is based upon.

It is senseless to hope that someone else will take care of our life for us. Do not hope that the government, political parties, a certain representative or sponsors will take care of you. You are the only owner of your life, and therefore, you should take care of it. Your life is predictable, if you know the laws of life and live according to them.

If you go to church, then you are lucky because through the church and fellowship with other believers, you can receive new knowledge, God's wisdom, and inspiration. However, do not hope that the church will completely take care of you. That is a wrong position - the dependent's position. You get the right motivation in the church to direct your energy toward achieving success, so that by moving forward you can attain your set goal. The church can teach you how to fulfill your destiny with enthusiasm, excellence, and victory mentality. However, you are the one to move toward the goal. Nobody will do this for you. Nobody will live your life for you.

Believers, with the help of God, are capable of creating their future themselves. Their lives can be predictable. However, they must never forget the Lord after attaining their peak of success.

...But remember the LORD your God, for it is he who gives you the ability to produce wealth, and so confirms his covenant, which he swore to your forefathers, as it is today.

Deuteronomy 8:18

According to this Scripture, you will have to acquire riches yourself. God does not give success and riches to man. He gives the power (the ability) to get them. He gives strength to work on attaining success and acquiring riches.

God promises to give us power; the power of decision, idea, inspiration, wisdom and knowledge. He promises to give us power in all the spheres of our lives so that we could get everything necessary for fulfilling our calling. God gives us power not only to meet our needs, but to establish the Kingdom of God on earth. He gives us everything necessary to make it in life and to fulfill our destiny. He reveals the secrets of life to us in His Word, so that we could create our future ourselves.

There are several principles of creating your future, and we will examine this below.

The first principle. Nothing will change in your life until you make a firm decision about what you want to specifically achieve. You cannot create your future, if you do not have a purpose; if there is no concrete life goal. For example, I have a goal to win this world for Jesus Christ. Everything else in my life is subject to this goal. I know what I will do in the future - in the next 5, 10, 15 years. My life has already been planned ahead of time. My life is not a mystery to me; it is predictable because I know precisely that I am the only one who should create it together with God and according to His will. There-fore, I purposefully work on bringing Christ's influence to all the spheres of society. For His sake, I am ready to turn this world upside down and show it that there is an alternative to regular human existence. There is another meaningful life - a life with God, a life dedicated only to Him.

I work diligently daily, aspiring to achieve my goal and establish the Kingdom of our Lord Jesus Christ on earth, so that it would become the Kingdom of this world. The "embassy of the Blessed Kingdom of God," is one of the largest evangelical churches in Europe, but it is not my main goal. It is just a way (a means) to achieve the main purpose of my life.

Define your goal, which should be in accordance with your calling. It should not be some mercantile purpose, it should be a purpose, which pleases God and is according to His will for your life. It should be a very important purpose, which you are ready to devote your whole life to, regardless of what it would cost you.

The second principle. Everything in your life should be subject to the main purpose of life. There are too many distracting moments in this world - offers, hobbies, purchases, etc. However, if you want to create your future according to God's will, then make a firm decision to make everything subject to the goal you have set before yourself!

If you want to please God and leave your mark in the history of mankind, then be focused on the main goal of your life. Let all your passion and heart be geared toward this purpose. Your purpose should not be above God in your life. The highest place in your life should always belong to Him. Only on this condition, will He help you to achieve your purpose by revealing to you the secrets of how to get to the peak of success in life.

The third principle. Touch your vision daily; touch your goal and purpose daily. Do something little-by-little to come closer to your goal. A proverb says, "The journey of a thousand miles begins with one small step." Therefore, steadily move forward toward your goal, not missing a day. If you can do nothing physically about your goal today, then at least pray or study something, but try to do something every day toward fulfilling your vision. Though gently, daily move forward in fulfilling your vision. Make concrete efforts to attain your goal and make it become a reality.

It is impossible to attain the big goal God sets before you, in one day, or automatically. This is what stops many people who have great dreams and purpose from attaining them. They are stopped because they are frightened because their set goal is very big, their vision is so huge, and they need a great amount of time and efforts to fulfill this purpose. This makes them to start doubting the reality of fulfilling such plan, forgetting that there is nothing impossible with God, who gave the vision to them.

A big vision needs to be divided into smaller parts; then you need to plan how to execute them in time, and start moving forward, gradually achieving more new pinnacles. In other words, every one of us needs to learn to divide great goals into intermediate ones, which are smaller in size. Fulfilling intermediate goals will not be a great problem for us.

The fourth principle. Make a decision never to return to your former condition of idleness, poverty or weakness. Move forward, forgetting all the bad things that happened to you in the past, and move toward the purpose where God's reward is waiting for you. Making such a decision and constantly moving forward toward the purpose will definitely get you to your set goal. However, staying in one place and doing nothing will lead you to attaining nothing.

There may be temptations, obstacles and difficulties on your way. Perhaps, you may want to quit and relax if you are not seeing the results of your labor. However, do not give in to this, simply force yourself to move forward at any cost. Small result is a result too. The small fruit will get bigger if you do not give up. Therefore, do not neglect small results.

Make a decision not to remain on the level where you are now, and not to return to where you came from. Always move forward ever. Do not remain in the place where life has thrown you.

Today many people complain that life is unfair to them. Those who count on the justice of life will surely be disappointed because everything depends on us, not on life. The sense of life depends only on every one of us.

Before demanding justice from life, we need to know the established laws and rules of life. It is necessary to know the principles by which life works because only by observing these principles can we count on life to be favorable to us.

It would be naive to expect, that by breaking all life systems, it is possible to achieve something in this life. Life does not become wonderful automatically. Life is fair only to those, who treat it well. Therefore, it is not worth engaging in self-deception or having some illusions. Life will treat you according to how you observe its rules and principles. Sometimes, it may seem very harsh and unfair, but the main thing is how you react to it. What will be your attitude toward the different seasons of life?

For example, if you were offended or disappointed by a person, whom you repeatedly helped, how will you treat him? Will you return insult for insult? Will you hide your grudges, and never again want to greet him? How will you react in similar situations? Will you be led by your feelings and emotions, or by the laws of life in every situation?

When you find yourself in difficult circumstances of life, do you think of how Jesus Christ would react to the same circumstance, if He was in your position? He should be our example in everything because He perfectly knew all the laws, principles and rules of life. The recommendations that the Lord gives us through the Bible are the correct principles upon which life is built. If we live by God's principles, life will be fair to us and success will always be on our side.

It is not so easy to observe the principles of life because they often contradict the human logic we are used to. For example, Jesus Christ says:

> **...Do not repay anyone evil for evil. Be careful to do what is right in the eyes of everybody. If it is possible, as far as it depends on you, live at peace with everyone. Do not take revenge, my friends, but leave**

room for God's wrath, for it is written: "It is mine to avenge; I will repay," says the Lord. On the contrary: "If your enemy is hungry, feed him; if he is thirsty, give him something to drink. In doing this, you will heap burning coals on his head." Do not be overcome by evil, but overcome evil with good.

Romans 12:17-21

...Do not repay evil with evil or insult with insult, but with blessing, because to this you were called so that you may inherit a blessing. For, whoever would love life and see good days must keep his tongue from evil and his lips from deceitful speech. He must turn from evil and do good; he must seek peace and pursue it....

1 Peter 3:9-11

At first sight, it seems that if we relate to life using these principles, people will simply laugh at us. However, people's opinion is only important to those who do not know God. The person who has a personal relationship with Him, is totally indifferent to what people think of him or her. The most important thing is what the Lord thinks about every one of us.

God's principles are absolutely true. The truth is always right; observing it guarantees us victory in life. Truth is eternal, it is impossible to destroy it. That is why nobody can dispute God's laws. These laws rule the world and human relationships regardless of whether we agree with them and observe them or not. They are established forever and exist absolutely independently from our opinion about them.

However, very often we either do not know these principles and consequently do not observe them, or we do not trust them. We simply do not have faith that these laws are truly supreme. Often we do not believe that God is a God of justice. We do not believe that God, by all means will do what He says He will do. We do not believe that the final word is always the Lord's because His word is established in heaven. Therefore, often we do not rely on God's laws, we live by human customs and laws, and as a result, we lose God's blessings.

THE RESPONSIBILITY FOR LIFE

It is easier for people to accuse others for their failures, the injustice of life, other people's wrong attitude toward them than to honestly admit their own mistakes and blunders. However, only we ourselves must bear the responsibility for our life. The Bible says:

So then, each of us will give an account of himself to God.

Romans 14:12

Only we ourselves are responsible for the life which is given to us by God. Therefore, we should realize that the full responsibility for the way we live, and how successful we are in life, is given to us by God. No one else is entitled to manage it, and at the same time no one else will be accountable for it. We ourselves are responsible for our life on earth. That is why we cannot allow ourselves to be led by the opinion of other people, who will not answer for us before God. The full responsibility for the way we have spent our life time on earth is only on us.

In other words, the destiny of each person is in his own hands. There is nothing new in the fact that evil rules the world in which we live. The Bible warns us about life with these words:

We know that we are children of God, and that the whole world is under the control of the evil one.

1 John 5:19

While the devil is in control of earthly matters, there is nothing surprising in what is happening on earth. Therefore, nothing should surprise and shock us because what is happening in this evil world is the will of the devil. It is a normal condition in the kingdom of darkness.

Jesus Christ came to this earth in order to destroy the works of the devil and to establish God's just laws, the laws of the Kingdom of God. These laws must determine the life of those, who are already in the Kingdom. Thanks to the saving sacrifice of Jesus Christ, you and I, as children of God, should not be living under the laws, which used to control our lives before we came to God. Now, as full-fledged citizens of the Kingdom of God, we should build our lives according to the laws, which are established in this Kingdom.

We should not expect that everything will be straight and smooth in this life. We are not in heaven yet, we are still here on earth. Very often, people will treat us not the way we would like to be treated. However, we should always remember the fact that our life is not determined by the evil, which someone does against us personally or against other people. Our reaction to this evil is what determines our life.

For example, I was raised by my grandmother, who I considered my mother in my childhood. I never saw my father. This could have harden my heart and force me to complain about life. Certainly, I always wanted to have a normal family just like my peers. I was curious to know why my father did not live with my mother, whom I, by the way, saw for the first time only when I was 12 years old because she remarried and lived separately.

Of course, in my childhood, I needed my parents. I needed their care, love and attention. However, when I came to God, I completely stopped thinking about it, I stopped feeling incomplete and rejected. I simply found a father in Him, and since then, as an obedient son, I tried to carry out His instructions. I am confident that all rules and laws that are established by Him are for my good. They are established specifically to make my life successful, joyful and happy because the father loves me very much, and wishes me only good.

People in our society are used to complaining about everybody and blaming others for their problems. That is how those who do not want to take responsibility for their life act. Those, who either do not know the laws of life, or refuse to live in accordance with them, behave exactly like that.

God knows perfectly how we are made and the laws we should live by to make our lives meaningful. He knows that we are created in order to live by the laws of love, optimism and positive thinking. God knows that evil and hatred are disastrous for us. As soon as we start living by the laws of hatred, our bodies will start destroying itself because hatred is unnatural to us.

We are created after God's nature - the nature of love. God has created us in His image and likeness. He is love, and He created us for love. Therefore, the most important laws, which we should live by, are the laws of love. The two main commandments given by Jesus Christ are to determine the foundation on which our life is being built. Here is what the Bible says about this:

> **One of them, an expert in the law, tested him with this question: "Teacher, which is the greatest commandment in the Law?" Jesus replied: "Love the Lord your God with all your heart and with all your soul and with all your mind." This is the first and greatest commandment. And the second is like it: "Love your neighbor as yourself." All the Law and the Prophets hang on these two commandments.**

Mathew 22:35-40

Not just someone out there needs this love, but personally each one of us needs such love. Only in this condition can we function the way God originally planned for us. Otherwise, hatred will destroy us. This is the way God's laws work. We cannot live against the laws of God and expect that all will be well with us. Commandments, that is, laws, are established by God for our good and for our well-being.

God tells us to love even our enemies. Not because they are worthy of our love, but only because when we feel hatred toward them, we ourselves suffer first, destroying our own life. It is impossible to live a normal way, if we act against the principles and the laws of God.

So what should we do to begin a new life - the life in accordance with God's laws? In a nut shell, there are only two conditions. The first one is to know the principles of God and the second one is to strictly observe them. However, it can never be over emphasized that to live by God's laws, it is necessary to have certain skills and develop new habits. Therefore, I want to give you some advice on how to start your life again, from the scratch.

- First of all, turn to God in prayer and tell Him about all your problems and hardships: about everything that worries and disturbs you today. Indeed, Jesus says:

Come to me, all you who are weary and burdened, and I will give you rest. Take my yoke upon you and learn from me, for I am gentle and humble in heart, and you will find rest for your souls. For my yoke is easy and my burden is light.

Mathew11:28-30

God wants you to give all of your problems to Him, and not try to solve them by yourself. Truly, sometimes our problems are too much for us to handle. For this very reason apostle Peter advises you:

Cast all your anxiety on him because he cares for you.

1 Peter 5:7

Do not worry about anything; simply try to do what the Lord tells you.

- Ask God to give you a dream, a vision and a goal that is worth living for. In other words, you need to find your destiny, the reason why you are saved and called by God. Every one of us has a mission on earth; we all have a task from God. We were given life on earth to fulfill this task. Life without a purpose is simply a meaningless existence. God is the only one who can reveal the purpose of our lives to us. To achieve this purpose, we were given certain abilities and talents. As we fellowship with God, we should find out our destiny, in order to successfully carry it out. However, we will not be able to do so without having first studied the laws of life.

- Make a decision; learn to react to every of life's situation in the right way. Remember, it does not matter what is happening to you, but what matters is the way you react to it. It is necessary to learn to take any failure in life - as a hint, as a possibility to do things in a different way. Remember the fact that there is a law of the flip side of a coin; therefore, God will definitely turn any problem into our good.

- Work in such a way, that you would be the best wherever you are. Do everything as unto the Lord, and then you will be able to reach the apex of success. Be zealous and diligent at work, and then God will begin to lift you up. Try to always do more than others, attain maximum success in your business of fulfilling God's purpose and glorify His name on earth.

- Constantly acquire new knowledge, practice self-education. Remember that only those who have more information rule the modern world.

- Always do good to people. Regardless of how the people around you treat you - treat them with love. Do good, and it will come back to you in a thousand fold; indeed, a man reaps what he sows.

- Make a decision to be a conqueror in life. Never give up. Even if you have fallen, get up and move on. Conquerors never surrender; therefore, be strong and courageous during tests, and firmly believe that together with God, you are invincible in this life.

You do not have limitations in life, except the limitations of your mind.

Every person's life must be planned. It must be predictable. The person, who does not plan his life, basically plans to fail. If a person does not have a purpose in life, he will never achieve anything. If you are not planning for any results, you will not achieve them.

By planning all the spheres of our lives, we can pray that God would help us in their realization. In this way, we create in the spiritual realm, what we plan to have in the material world in the future. This has to do with our job and career, our family and our children's future, our financial well-being and our ministry. In every sphere of our lives we must have clear and concrete plans. Only by doing so can we have breakthroughs and achieve success in life. Otherwise our lives will be full of various chances, which will never allow us to have a meaningful life.

Unfortunately, many Christians think that they should not plan their life. However, our God is God of planning. The whole Old Testament reveals to us God's plan about Jesus Christ's coming to earth. Every book of the Old Testament prophesied about Jesus, predicting His birth and ministry.

Prophecy is a plan. We see that in the words of the great prophet Isaiah:

See, the former things have taken place, and new things I declare; before they spring into being I announce them to you.

Isaiah 42:9

Isaiah mentions that what was said before (that is, planned earlier) have taken place. God does not do anything on this earth, without first revealing His plan to the people through His prophets.

Surely the Sovereign LORD does nothing without revealing his plan to his servants the prophets.

Amos 3:7

Just like God, we should plan our life by listening to His advice in everything. Our life should be predictable and then, no occasions will be able to draw us back on our way to attaining success in achieving our life's purpose.

There is nothing impossible for us. If something does not work out in life, there is only one reason for that:

we do not have sufficient information in that particular field. We do not know what God thinks about that issue. Our mind is limited, and the lack of necessary knowledge does not give us an opportunity to move forward.

If you fulfill God's will, then God will always be your ally. He wants to use you in order to establish His Kingdom on earth. We must have plans in order to know how to fulfill God's idea.

For example, our church "The embassy of the Blessed Kingdom of God" has specific plan for fulfilling God's intention for the salvation of the people of Ukraine. We know the number of people we have to bring to God in this country. In addition, we also know how many people we have to bring to God throughout the world. Our missionary activities are planned based on this. We precisely know when and what we have to do to fulfill this plan we are responsible for before God.

Every one of us is God's weapon in this world. We are tools in God's hand. He wants to use us to keep this world from decay and total destruction. This is not some sort of self-exaltation, or an unhealthy desire to be great, but a fact. We, Christians, are the chosen people, who are called to fulfill the great plan of God - establishing His Kingdom on earth. Every one of us has his own part in fulfilling this plan and God has already prepared everything we need for its fulfillment in life.

His divine power has given us everything we need for life and godliness through our knowledge of him who called us by his own glory and goodness. Through these he has given us his very great and precious prom-

**ises, so that through them you may partic-
ipate in the divine nature and escape the
corruption in the world caused by evil
desires.**

2 Peter 1:3,4

Dear reader, you may want to object that everything has been given to you. This may seem unreal to you. However, I would like to tell you that it is necessary to have patience, and grow in the knowledge of God. This will definitely bring you to the point, where you will be fully engaged and you will be able to receive all God's blessings intended for you.

Every important thing you need for your life has already been given to you: these are not material things at all. The most important three human needs are peace and rest of the soul, health and happiness. All these great assets are already given to us by God. People, who live by the customs of the world badly need all of these. Their lives are full of worry, diseases and grief. Christians have an enormous advantage because they live in peace, joy and health. All of these are given to us not just for our lives, but for life and godliness. We are given all of these so that we could live a godly life on this earth.

Everything is given to you, but maybe today you do not have anything. What is the root of the problem? The problem is that you do not know what God knows. Your knowledge does not correspond to God's knowledge!

For example, God knows how you can achieve success. However, if you cannot call yourself a successful person, it means what God knows has not been revealed to you. You do not know God's laws for achieving success. God said that He will fulfill your needs according to His riches. Then why do you experience serious financial difficulties? The answer is still the same: your mind is limited due to the absence of necessary information, which is available in God. God knows how you can become rich, but you do not know the laws of financial prosperity.

It is only by getting to know God, by growing in the knowledge of His laws and principles, that we can remove the limitations that exist in our mind and prevent us from revealing God on earth and fulfill His plan. Focus your attention on how you can receive everything that God has already given to you. Let us carefully investigate the Scripture mentioned above.

His divine power has given us everything we need for life and godliness <u>through our knowledge</u> of him who called us by his own glory and goodness. Through these he has given us his very great and precious promises, so that through them you may participate in the divine nature and escape the corruption in the world caused by evil desires.

2 Peter 1:3,4 (underlined by the author)

Everything is given to us through "the knowledge!" The knowledge of God and the knowledge of what He knows. Therefore, every one of us needs to constantly go deeper into getting to know God, His laws and principles, which are revealed in His Word. The more we get to know Him, the more opportunities we will have, and the more the thing given to us by God will be manifested in our lives.

You should seek God in every direction of your life, in order to obtain from Him the knowledge necessary for you. If your outlooks on life correspond with the way the Lord sees it, then you will know exactly what, when and how you should do things to successfully fulfill your destiny, God's plan for your life. Knowing this plan, you will not live "blindly." Your life will be predictable because it will be devoted to God, and guided by His laws and principles.

Everything we need for a meaningful life already exists in Jesus Christ. Everything has been given to us! However, the real manifestation of it depends only on our knowledge of God and His laws of life.

Enlarge the limits of your mind by getting to know God and His truths - and you will become a person who do not have any limitations in life. Every one of us can become whatever he wants to be. Every one of us can achieve incredible success in life. The life of every one of us can be predictable. All we need for this is to take any limitations off our mind, by filling it with knowledge of what God knows, the knowledge of His laws and principles. Observing this will make our lives be like it was originally planned to be by God.

EVERYTHING IS EXPOSED BY THE LIGHT

As mentioned above, everything has already been given to us by God in order for our lives to be successful and meaningful. However, God's Word says,

But everything exposed by the light becomes visible, for it is light that makes everything visible.

Ephesians 5:13,14

There is a very deep thought concealed in this Scripture. Knowledge is light. Everything manifesting from the nonexistence, from the invisible spiritual realm, becomes real in this physical world through exposure by the light, or knowledge. Speaking in other words, it means everything has already been given to us in Jesus Christ. However, it will not become a reality in our life without specific knowledge.

Darkness, that is, ignorance, limits our visibility. It conceals things that are visible from us. It is light (knowledge) that exposes everything. Light reveals to us the right way to success which was hidden in darkness from us. Getting to know Christ always brings positive changes in the life of a man. This is why we all should constantly grow in the knowledge of the Lord, and His laws of life. Then, the light of His truth will increasingly illuminate all spheres of our lives, and only then can our life become predictable.

Breakthrough is guaranteed if there is enough light. Success will be in the place where God's light is shining. God does not have hopeless situations because He is the light. He has knowledge. If we have this knowledge of God, then victory in all spheres of life is guaranteed to us.

THE SECRET OF DANIEL'S ELEVATION

Daniel was a wise prophet of God, who though was a captive, became very successful and close to the king.

To these four young men God gave knowledge and understanding of all kinds of literature and learning. And Daniel could understand visions and dreams of all kinds. At the end of the time set by the king to bring them in, the chief official presented them to Nebuchadnezzar. The king talked with them, and he found none equal to Daniel, Hananiah, Mishael and Azariah; so they entered the king's service. In every matter of wisdom and understanding about which the king questioned them, he found them ten times better than all the magicians and enchanters in his whole kingdom.

Daniel 1:17-20

What was the wisdom that made this man successful and respected in the society based on? Daniel studied many books. He has been meditating upon them for a long time. He had a wide range of knowledge. However, what made him different from the Babylonian youths, who also had a wide range of knowledge in various spheres of life, was that Daniel with his friends, Hananiah, Mishael, and azariah, have also been studying God's laws.

The secret of Daniel's elevation is this: he studied everything the world has to offer, and added the knowledge of God's law to it. This divine knowledge secured a high social status for Daniel, who was just a prisoner in a foreign country. The powerful king of the great Babylon - Nebuchadnezzar - has been listening to his opinion on various vital matters. Daniel knew what God knew, and it made him ten times smarter than all the wise men of the Babylonian Kingdom. This determined his position in life.

What was accessible to Daniel, back then, is accessible to anybody, who follows Jesus Christ today. We have free access to the wisdom of God, His knowledge, which will guarantee us a successful life. We have free access to the knowledge of His laws, which will make our life completely predictable.

The Bible says,

Every prudent man acts out of knowledge, but a fool exposes his folly.

Proverbs 13:16

Every one of us should keep in mind the fact that the attempt to start doing something without first studying the subject and acquiring the necessary knowledge from God is exposing our foolishness. A prudent person longs to acquire the knowledge of the Scriptures, on which this life on earth is built upon.

No one will rise above what he knows. We need to know God and His laws in order to have a meaningful life. This is what will give us the opportunity to fulfill our destiny on earth successfully.

You are the one who decides where you will be tomorrow. The position we are holding today is our personal responsibility. Who we are today and the kind of life we are living depends only on us. Definitely it is a lot easier to blame someone else (our loved ones, friends, bosses or government) for our failures and hardships. However, if we will be honest with ourselves, then we would recognize the fact that no one else, apart from us, is guilty of not yet attaining success in our life.

Whatever happens to us is our responsibility, therefore, we should never grumble and complain, but simply try to realize that we should learn to take responsibility for our lives. We should learn to make important decisions. It is essential to learn the laws of life for our life to become predictable.

Everything that happens to us today is solely a result of the decisions we made yesterday. Our decisions yesterday determine the conditions we are in today. What we will have tomorrow and the day after tomorrow depend on the principles and the laws of life we observe today. Breakthrough in life is possible tomorrow, only for those people who are making use of the principles of prosperity, success, zeal, diligence, persistence and diligence in their life today.

Many believers simply expect miracles, but these miracles can take place only if you observe specific laws of God. If you do not do anything while expecting miracles, then there is no reason to complain, grumble or blame God, if the miracles do not come. You yourself have contributed to the problems, poverty and failures in your life by not doing anything. You did not observe any principles and did nothing toward having the prosperity you dreamed so much about. You did not do anything toward achieving promotion, which you are praying about. You did not do anything concrete in this world that is subject to specific laws. Without this, your expectation of wonderful changes in life will not be satisfied.

You have to start doing something in specific spheres of your life, where you want to attain success. If you are praying about promotion, then change your attitude toward your job and start doing something that you have not been doing before.

Study what the word of God (His law) has to say about the sphere of life, where you desire to see a breakthrough. For example, if you want to have financial prosperity, then try to find out as much as possible truth about what the Bible has to say about it. God says:

Lazy hands make a man poor, but diligent hands bring wealth.

Proverbs 10:4

God has precisely determined what is needed for your financial prosperity. Note, that He does not indicate that the only thing you should do is to pray. He says, that you should be diligent at work; therefore do not expect financial changes if you are not diligent at work! Moreover, it is not worth expecting changes in your financial condition, if you do not have any job. If you are not complying with God's word, (His principle) then no prayer will help you.

God would rather bless a diligent unbeliever than a lazy believer because His laws are firm. The one who observes the law will definitely be blessed. In other words,

God commends obedience to His principles more than empty prayers not supported by any works.

HAPPINESS IS NOT IN WHAT YOU HAVE

A truly successful person is a happy person. But what is happiness? Happiness is not in what you have. It does not depend on the amount of money in your bank account, or the material properties you possess. What then is happiness?

In actual fact, happiness is in what you do with what you have. Happiness will come into your life only when you use what God has given you to manage in the best way. Even if you do not have a lot, begin using what you have in the right way and thank God for it.

Often the problem of many people is that they concentrate too much on what they do not have. This becomes the reason for disappointment, depression, constant complaints and as a result, it leads to self-destruction.

Someone does not like his wife's figure; someone does not like her husband's hair-style; someone constantly complains about his neighbor, or boss at work; someone does not like the government, or the President of the country. Such people see only the negative side of life, and therefore their thinking is concentrated on negative thoughts.

The one who desires to achieve success and prosperity must be focused on positive things in life, on its advantages. This is truly what we should be constantly thankful to the Lord for, just as apostle Paul, who said,

But godliness with contentment is great gain.

1 Timothy 6:6

Stop complaining about the whole world! May complaint and grumble be eliminated from your life forever. Give thanks to God always and for everything, if you want to become a successful person and attain your goal.

Thus, happiness is not in what we have. Having a lot and with the best quality, does not necessarily speak about your success and happiness. If you do not have godliness and contentment, nothing in this life will make you happy.

How do you use what you already have today? Are you truly thankful to God? Are you fully benefiting God's Kingdom with everything that belongs to you? Every one of us needs to learn to be satisfied with what we have today. The reason for that is that one day in everyone's life there will be a moment, when we will not be satisfied with what we have. But we should learn to live with what we have and be grateful to God for it.

For example, one day whether you want it or not, your hair will become gray, and wrinkles will appear on your face. This is the law of nature. Maybe, once you had a big business, but today you hardly have enough money till the next paycheck. The important thing is not what you have, but your attitude toward it. Do you continue to thank God for everything you have, are you complaining and showing your dissatisfaction?

Everything we have today, even something small, should fully be used to serve God and people, continuously glorifying God in our hearts, against any odd.

Something big is never born suddenly. First, God wants us to learn the proper use of what we have. He wants us to have the right attitude, the right heart, right approach and understanding of what we have in our lives today. If our heart is full of appreciation to God, if we are contented by all He has already blessed us with, then by this we prove to God, that we are worthy to receive something better.

Usually, people have a lot of miserable problems, people get accustomed to worrying about insignificant issues. It is not worth worrying about something you do not have. Exclude it from the list of your worries, and all your problems will be solved 90% immediately. For this very reason, Jesus Christ said that we should not worry about anything. It is against the law of nature, against the laws of life to worry. God knows what we really need, and He will never be slow in helping you.

Your life and your tomorrow are secured in God. Do everything possible for God today, and He will take care of your tomorrow. God knows what you need and what will ruin you. He knows what is harmful to you, and what will disgrace you. He loves you, and that is why He is not giving you what you are asking for persistently. Be thankful to God for what you have. Simply start enjoying the life.

Begin to notice those valuables, which you have. If what you have is not much, that is not a sufficient reason to neglect it. If you do not thank God for it, if you do not worship Him for it, you are simply offending and insulting Him.

What did Moses have? He had just a rod, a usual stick. Moses did not have money or his own army, he had no influence, but He had to go against Pharaoh. It seems like a crazy idea. Normally, to go against the powerful Pharaoh of Egypt, you had to exceed him in strength and might. Moses had almost nothing, but He was grateful to God for what He had, he used it fully for the glory of God. Moses understood the importance of what he had. Secondly, he did not neglect what he had. He was ready to fully use the little that he possessed.

And guess what? God used Moses' rod in such a way that through that rod, a stick from the tree, He delivered a whole nation. If you think that you do not have anything, remember Moses. Use the little that God has given you, and you will receive much more.

Sometimes we do not realize the value of what we have. What did Joseph, Daniel and David have? They did not have anything remarkable, but each of them had courage, persistence, perseverance and the desire to please God. In addition to that, each of them had the knowledge of the laws of life; therefore they always calmly face life's challenges and problems. Their lives were predictable for them because they were constantly longing to know God and His laws.

Happiness is not in having a lot of everything. Happiness is in creating your happiness with your own hands.

Thus, do not ever worry about what you cannot change, about things that do not depend on you. Begin doing something that you can do. Focus your attention on what you can, and grow in it. Do it the best way you can - and God will enlarge your opportunities and remove the limitations. The main thing is this: constantly grow in knowing God and His laws of life. Then life will become predictable for you, and it will open the way to achieve success in fulfilling your calling, for the sake of which He has granted you this life.

GOLDEN TRUTHS

- The knowledge of the laws of life makes life predictable.
- The future of every one of us is in our own hands.
- Nobody will live your life for you.
- You cannot create your future, if you do not have a purpose.
- Everything in your life should be subject to the main purpose of life.
- Your purpose should not be above God in your life.
- Touch your vision daily.
- Having begun, constantly move forward toward your goal, and you will definitely attain your goal.
- Life will treat you according to how you observe its rules and principles.
- Truth is always right, observing it guarantees us victory in life.
- The person who does not plan his life is basically planning to fail.
- If you fulfill God's will, then God will always be your friend.
- Darkness, that is, ignorance, limits our visibility.
- Breakthrough is guaranteed, if there is enough light.
- No one will rise above what he knows.

If you have not yet accepted Jesus Christ as your Lord and Savior, I am inviting you right now to speak to Him in prayer. God will give you true joy, peace and happiness. Only God can answer all your questions, He is the only One who can solve your problems. Live with God, have faith in God – it is true happiness. God loves you and He is waiting for you. He needs you.

SINNER'S PRAYER

Heavenly Father! I come to You in prayer, confessing all of my sins. I believe Your Word. I believe that You accept everyone who comes to You. Lord, forgive me all my sins, have mercy on me. I don't want to live this way anymore. I want to belong to You, Jesus! Come into my heart and cleanse me. Be my Savior and my Pastor. Guide me. I confess You, Jesus Christ as my Lord. I thank You that You hear my prayer and I accept my salvation by faith. I thank You, my Savior, for accepting me just as I am.
Amen.

If you sincerely prayed this prayer, God heard you and forgave you all your sins. Now, God is your Father, and Jesus is your Friend. Read the Word, live with God and pray.

The Holy Spirit - is the third Personality of the Divine Trinity. He is the One, who the Father sent to be with His children. The Holy Spirit convicts us when we do something wrong, He guides us back to the right path. Very often we grieve Him. When we find ourselves in difficult situations, trying to sort what is right and what is wrong. He helps us by shedding His light on our situation, if we are in tune with Him. The Holy Spirit will teach you, how to distinguish between right and wrong doctrines. He will help you to find a church, where Jesus Christ is exalted.

PRAYER FOR BAPTISM IN THE HOLY SPIRIT

Now, I am born again. I am a Christian. I am a child of the Almighty God! I am saved! Lord, You said in your Word: **"If ye then, being evil, know how to give gifts unto your children: how much more shall your Heavenly Father give the Holy Spirit to them that ask him?"** *(Luke 11:13). I plead with You, Lord fill me with the Holy Spirit. Holy Spirit rise up in me, when I praise You. I believe that I will speak in an unknown language.*
Amen.

SUNDAY ADELAJA'S
BIOGRAPHY

Pastor Sunday Adelaja is the Founder and Senior Pastor of The Embassy of the Blessed Kingdom of God for All Nations Church in Kyiv, Ukraine.

Sunday Adelaja is a Nigerian-born Leader, Thinker, Philosopher, Transformation Strategist, Pastor, Author and Innovator who lives in Kiev, Ukraine.

At 19, he won a scholarship to study in the former Soviet Union. He completed his master's program in Belorussia State University with distinction in journalism.

At 33, he had built the largest evangelical church in Europe — The Embassy of the Blessed Kingdom of God for All Nations.

Sunday Adelaja is one of the few individuals in our world who has been privileged to speak in the United Nations, Israeli Parliament, Japanese Parliament and the United States Senate.

The movement he pioneered has been instrumental in reshaping lives of people in the Ukraine, Russia and about 50 other nations where he has his branches.

His congregation, which consists of ninety-nine percent white Europeans, is a cross-cultural model of the church for the 21st century.

His life mission is to advance the Kingdom of God on earth by

raising a generation of history makers who will live for a cause larger, bigger and greater than themselves. Those who will live like Jesus and transform every sphere of the society in every nation as a model of the Kingdom of God on earth.

His economic empowerment program has succeeded in raising over 200 millionaires in the short period of three years.

Sunday Adelaja is the author of over 300 books, many of which are translated into several languages including Russian, English, French, Chinese, German, etc.

His work has been widely reported by world media outlets such as The Washington Post, The Wall Street Journal, New York Times, Forbes, Associated Press, Reuters, CNN, BBC, German, Dutch and French national television stations.

Pastor Sunday is happily married to his "Princess" Bose Dere-Adelaja. They are blessed with three children: Perez, Zoe and Pearl.